'Bishop I want you to know that we have become Christians through our Alpha Group. I also want you to know that our son is gay and we have learnt more about the true meaning of love from his experience.' A phone call out of the blue over 10 years ago. It is time for the church to catch up with the experience of its own members.

These essays are long overdue. They are rooted in a deep respect for difference and diversity, in mutual and transparent pastoral love, in a fresh and vibrant wrestling with the Scriptures and Christian tradition and they rescue the Church from the real threat that it will be stranded in a culture that belongs to the past. The authors have listened and learnt and are still travelling on. So must we!

Rt Rev John Gladwin, former Bishop of Chelmsford

As someone who is passionate about the importance of listening to different perspectives in places of intense disagreement, I welcome these honest contributions to the debate about same sex relationships -- regardless of whether they disturb or comfort us. This book invites us to engage prayerfully with the personal stories of fellow followers of Christ; to listen deeply with hearts of love not fear; and to know that God is unchanged whatever our conclusions.

Rt Rev Rachel Treweek, Bishop of Gloucester

Much has and, no doubt, will continue to be stated in regards to evangelical understanding of sexuality. Sadly, especially for those whose lives are directly affected by the ever present commentary, the voices are often raised and adamant. A set stance appears to be the 'positioning' claimed as the evangelical understanding of all that is around us at present.

That's why I welcome *Journeys in Grace and Truth*, which reveals a growing evangelical voice that needs to be heard and respected. Conversation by its very nature is (at least) two-way, and so I pray that as evangelicals we will hear well, and position less, as we seek together to share the hope-filled story of Jesus in this generation.

Ruth Gilson, CEO Girls' Brigade Ministries

I warmly welcome this book. These contributions seek to help Christians with different points of view in a very difficult debate. The authors seek to explain how sisters and brothers in the church can hold an affirming biblical evangelical view which embraces all LGBTI Christians. I know how difficult, divisive and painful th̶e̶s̶e̶ i̶ ̶ ̶ ̶ ̶ ̶ ̶ ̶ ̶ ̶ ̶ ̶ e̶ should all

welcome thoughtful contributions like this one as heralds of a new time of respectful dialogue and deeper understanding.

Rt Hon Sir Simon Hughes, former MP, Liberal Democrat Deputy Leader and Minister of State for Justice and Civil Liberties

I had the extraordinary privilege of participating as one of the Diocese's delegates in the 'Shared Conversations'. The most transformative experience for me was the session when we told our stories, of how we each had reached the point of view we were holding in relation to sexuality. The journeys were varied, multi-dimensional, contextual, and deeply faithful. Listening to such personal perspectives where individual faithfulness has lead us to such different places, it left me wondering by what route we might be able to find ourselves in the same place, or at least in places closer by. It also left me realising that was in God's hands not ours. It is for us to listen to each other in faith. Now this powerful collection of stories has strengthened that sense for me: listen in faith, and this is in God's hands.

Rt Rev Martin Seeley, Bishop of St Edmundsbury and Ipswich

Until very recently attitudes towards same sex relationships, not least among Christians, were seen by those like myself who study church statistics, to be a 'generational' issue. These were not matters on which adults tended to change their minds. Societal change only took place to the extent that those reaching adulthood differed from the generation they were replacing. Since the middle of the last decade that has all changed. This book collects together a range of examples of such a reassessment of views. In doing so it provides a very timely contribution to the Shared Conversations taking place within the Church of England. It is not the last or only word on the subject, but it is an essential one.

Rt Rev David Walker, Bishop of Manchester

Serious issues need serious debate, but as part of that debate it's important to hear of the journeys that people are making. Doubtless these journeys criss-cross the well-worn territory in many different directions but my hope is that when we meet on those journeys we will recognise fellow disciples of integrity and faithfulness. Here in this resource are some of those disciples telling their stories and asking only for an honest hearing. May we live in peace and proclaim Jesus Christ crucified and risen.

Rt Rev John Pritchard, former Bishop of Oxford

For all who are struggling
to reconcile their faith with their sexuality,
know that you are fearfully and wonderfully made
and that you are loved beyond measure.

JOURNEYS IN GRACE AND TRUTH

AND TRUTH

REVISITING SCRIPTURE AND SEXUALITY

JOURNEYS IN GRACE
AND TRUTH

REVISITING SCRIPTURE AND SEXUALITY

———— • ————

EDITED BY JAYNE OZANNE

Dear Maria

What a blessing to meet you,

Jayne

16/6/19

First published in 2016

This book is a Via Media publication under the full editorial control of ViaMedia.News (https://viamedia.news/)

Published on behalf of ViaMedia.News by:
Ekklesia
235 Shaftesbury Avenue
London
WC2H 8EP

Book Editor: Jayne Ozanne
Production and design: Bob Carling (www.carling.org.uk)
Editorial director for the publisher: Simon Barrow
Cover image: 'The Prodigal Daughter', by Charlie Mackesy

ISBN: 978-0-9932942-4-2

A Catalogue record for this book is available from the British Library.

Contents

EDITOR'S PREFACE

Nervously, he looked around him to check that we were truly alone, and then whispered: 'Jayne, I'm with you pastorally, honestly I *am*. It's just I'm not quite there theologically yet.'

I was grateful to him for his honesty, and indeed for his courage in risking being seen talking to me – for to do so ran the gauntlet of being labelled "unsound" by his colleagues. It had been ten years since we last met, and since I had last stepped foot into Church House. I had come back to reconnect with old friends who were still members of the Church of England's General Synod. It was all rather daunting and strange, and I could feel my heart pumping fast – my anxiety hidden behind a fixed smile. So much had changed (most notably within me!); so much was still exactly the same. The warren of corridors still provided secluded spots for people to have almost-private conversations, although you could never tell who you might bump into just around the corner – even an archbishop!

He ran a finger along the inside rim of his white dog-collar, which was attached to his bright blue shirt – typical evangelical attire – and tried to smile. It had been a difficult and painful conversation, for both of us. I had once again shared part of my journey from the intervening 'exile' years, a story that was so familiar to me in the telling that I forgot the impact it could often have on the listener.

He had known me well during my time on the Archbishops' Council, when I had been one of the six lay members appointed by the archbishops to bring some outside perspective and skills into the central Church structures. That had been a daring move back then in the 1990s, and one that had taken several years of debate in General Synod to approve. Of course, the Church does like to take its time over things, particularly if it might instigate unpredictable outcomes. And appointing six fresh voices into this august body of nineteen was seen as just that. As it turned out, most of the appointed members were already known to the Archbishops – but I most definitely was not, as indeed neither was the other 'young' member – David Lammy, who soon became the MP for Tottenham.

People used to ask me 'What was my "role" on Council?' I would always respond saying that whilst I had probably been appointed because I ticked various boxes (under 30 at the time of appointment; female; lay; charismatic Evangelical; a strategic management consultant who had worked in TV and international marketing), I thought my actual role was more akin to being the "Court Jester". By that I meant that I seemed to have landed the post of being the person who always named the "elephant in the room" – and so tried to lovingly speak the truth about what was happening in the Church. It meant I was seen as a trouble maker by many, but at the same time I made a group of new friends who were hungry for the Church to admit and address many of the difficulties that it was facing. That's why I pulled together a grand coalition of all the main mission agencies in order to produce the *Restoring Hope* video pack, which went to every parish church in the country. It was thanks to this, and other projects with which I was involved, that I became known to many as a leading Evangelical.

So when after years of private struggle and illness I finally chose to come out – it caused a bit of a stir.

I had kept my struggles regarding my sexuality to myself during my time on Council – believing that I had been healed of my 'unfortunate affliction'. Just a year before my appointment I had been rushed in to the Cromwell Hospital with undiagnosed chronic abdominal pain, which was closely followed by a breakdown. Years of privately trying to reconcile my faith and sexuality had finally had their toll. But even then I thought it was 'just a phase' I was going through, something I would 'grow out of' once I had got to the root cause of it all. Ten years later, when studying as a Visiting Research Fellow at Oxford University (looking at the impact of religion on international relations, thanks to my time alongside Canon Andrew White and Baroness Caroline Cox), I was once again rushed into hospital. This precipitated a second breakdown, and one which left me so utterly broken that even my close friends began to fear the worst. They knew, as I did, that I had tried everything I possibly could to 'rid myself' of my homosexual desires, and that I had also tried to live a life of enforced celibacy.

It was this lack of hope, knowing that I would never ever receive the intimacy and love that I so desperately longed for, that almost killed me. Make no mistake, it is a path which even Jesus says is 'only for those who can bear it'.[1] For me, it nearly cost me my life. I just couldn't understand that if God had made me the way he had,

---

1   Matthew 19:11

then why didn't he answer my prayer for grace to cope with it all?

So it seemed I only had one choice – and it was the most utterly terrifying choice of all. I *had* to find out who I was, and whether the love that I craved would actually bring me the joy and peace that I so desperately yearned for. In doing so, I believed I would be walking knowingly away from the light and into the dark, turning my back on the source of all Life and Love. It's difficult to put into words how sickeningly awful this made me feel, but I reckoned that God would somehow understand and love me "all the same" – a fallen sinner who was just trying to do the best she could to survive.

So I stepped out – and found that my wonderful loving beautiful Saviour was walking right with me!

He was there – just as he had *always* been. In the night hours, in the wakening hours, behind me, before me, around me and within. There in my waking and my sleeping. He just kept whispering to me, and his favour continued as it had always done. I very soon afterwards met someone who became the most important woman in my life to date, and we spent six incredible years together.

Peace, joy, happiness, love – the fruits were bountiful and plentiful, there for all to see.

I had had many (non-Evangelical) Christian friends who had urged me through the years to revisit Scripture on this issue, and to read more widely about how others interpreted those 'clobber' verses. I had point blank refused, because I *knew* what they said. Of course, I'd never actually (at that time) sat down and really *studied* them, but I knew what everyone around me believed – and they were all crystal clear and of one mind about it all. Homosexuality was a consequence of the sinful nature of the secular Western Society, and one that the true Bible-believing, God-fearing Church needed to faithfully stand against. Under no circumstance should we allow ourselves to be swayed. 'Stand firm, and hold fast to the teachings you have been taught'.[2] Don't let preachers of false doctrines turn you from the path – 'for the time will come when people will not put up with sound doctrine. Instead, to suit their own desires, they will gather around them teachers to suit what their itching ears want to hear. They will turn away their ears from listening

---

2 2 Thessalonians 2:15

to the truth and turn aside to myths'.[3] I knew these verses back-wards, not least because they were frequently quoted to me during prayer ministry times.

But maybe, just maybe these well-meaning Christian leaders were wrong? Maybe 'this' didn't mean 'that'? Maybe we were read-ing too much into the text, or indeed too little?

I started to read and research – thank heavens for the world wide web! I began to understand that there were indeed other ways of looking at and reading Scripture. For the first time, I began to tru-ly understand the patriarchal context in which Scripture had been written, and that as with the debate around women in leadership, we needed to understand that we have to take into account the so-cial context into which St Paul and others were speaking. I realised there was no mention at all about homosexual orientation in the Bible, and that the sexual acts described were more often than not in reference to temple prostitutes who used sex as a form of idol wor-ship – not as an expression of true intimacy between two individu-als who are deeply in love with each other. I then started to study the nature of desire, and saw how this stems from the fact that we are created in the image of God, who desires each one of us – indeed the greatest love affair of all, is that between Christ and His Church.

God *loves* us. Passionately. Unconditionally. There is nothing we can do to make him love us more. There is nothing we can do to make him love us less.

Full stop.

That is the whole point of Scripture – to reveal this wonderful incredible love, in the person of Jesus Christ. It may not be obvi-ous in the harsh realities of the Old Testament, but it is there all the same – constantly and consistently pointing towards Jesus Christ, 'who came to save life, not to destroy'.[4]

Jesus frequently encountered those who thought they knew the Bible better than he did, but with whom he kept engaging by pa-tiently explaining how they had 'missed the point'. *He* was there – right in front of their faces, and yet they couldn't see him. They had hardened their hearts to such a level that, believing so much in their own righteousness, they couldn't hear the deeper truth that he

3   2 Timothy 4: 2–4
4   Luke 9:56

wanted to share – that he is their Prince of Peace, the Lord of Life and the Lover of their Souls.

I have often reflected on that encounter with my friend at Synod who, rather like the nature of the meeting between Jesus and Nicodemus,[5] had felt it best to come and see me out of prying eyes' way.

How did we get to this place where Christians, especially Evangelicals, are fearful of saying what they truly think about this issue, which goes right to the core of what it is to be human? What road have we travelled that means that people who would willingly give their all for Christ, and frequently do, feel so afraid of publicly admitting that they've changed their mind for fear of being disowned by their colleagues and friends? Their tribe. The group to whom they belong, and get their affirmation.

I've lost count of the number of times people have whispered to me 'Jayne, I'm with you, I just can't say anything right now…I'm sorry'. I do understand the difficulty they are in – honestly, I do. But each time I hear it, it breaks my heart. It's not because I want their public support – although that would of course be helpful – but far more because it is yet further evidence of the fear that grips the heart of our Church, which keeps us fettered and keeps us from becoming all that God wants us to be.

And this, amongst a people who believe 'Perfect Love casts our Fear'![6]

Please know this – the voices of those who want to affirm LGBTI Christians for being who they are in Christ, and who want to recognise, bless and celebrate their monogamous, faithful, life-long unions, are growing. They are growing across the whole Church – including the 'Evangelical wing'.

They are all Christians who have a passion for truth, and who hold Scripture close to their hearts. They cannot be written off, or marginalised. They need to be heard, respected and recognised.

That's why I've commissioned this book. It's a collection of stories from leading Evangelicals within the Church of England, who I know hold – often after much soul searching and study – an affirming view. They have frequently come to this point of understanding

5   Cf John 3
6   1 John 4:18

in a 'fellowship vacuum', with very few people to talk to and at a great risk to themselves of being ridiculed and marginalised. But they have done so all the same – for they believe that that is what God has called them to do.

I salute their courage. They did not need to speak out, but they have each chosen to do so for they, like I, believe that the time has come for the Church to accept that there is more than one way of reading Scripture on this complex and vexed issue. The time for silence is over.

They are keen to provide a lead, and in so doing empower others to have the courage to speak out too. This is critically important as we enter a time of open discussion and dialogue within the Church.

Each of their journeys is intensely personal. Each is disarmingly honest. All grapple with Scripture.

I am particularly grateful to Marcus and Hayley who, like me, have openly shared their own private and painful struggles of coming to terms with their sexuality. They deserve great respect as they have done so in order that it may shed light on the challenge of being a gay Evangelical in today's Church.

So what do I hope this book will achieve?

Firstly, I hope it will bring hope and some element of healing to those who have been deeply wounded and scarred by the Church over this issue. If, like me, you have endured years of lonely heartache and pain, carrying a truth whose name you dare not even utter for fear of being rejected, please know you are dearly loved by the Beloved. I am sorry that the Church has not found a way of addressing this problem sooner, and I know that this will seem small succour for all that you've been through. Please know that in my mind you bear the stigmata of Christ – wounds inflicted by a Church that 'knows not what it does'. May you find it somehow in your heart to still cry 'Father Forgive', and to keep on loving this broken body that is trying to become the Bride of Christ.

Secondly, to those who have felt silenced – I pray that this book will encourage you to speak out and say what you truly believe, knowing that there are many others who believe as you do. There is no place for fear in our Church, not if we want to move forward into the fullness of what Christ has for us. It may be that you haven't come to a point of peace about everything yet, that's fine too, but the best way to address find peace is to talk about it with others who are also on a similar journey.

And finally, for those who have still to be convinced that there is actually another way of interpreting Scripture on this important issue, I pray that you will read this book with an open mind and an open heart. Do please ask that the Holy Spirit speaks to you as you read. Some of it will probably make you feel uncomfortable, I'm sure you will be used to that. Some of it may make you want to stop and put it down, in which case I ask you to persevere – for Love's sake. Some of it will leave you with questions, which I and others will be more than willing to answer, so please just ask.

The critical question for all of us, I believe, is to ask what is the Spirit saying to our Church today?

To answer that will require an open mind, a humble heart, and a level of brokenness that only comes from knowing how much we are loved, and how little we deserve it.

For whatever we think and feel on this issue, wherever we stand, I know that we are all called to obey the same commands and journey the same road, which as Jesus said are to 'love the Lord your God with all your heart, and with all of your soul and all of your mind … and to love your neighbour as yourself'.[7]

Grace and peace to you all.

Jayne Ozanne
Oxford
May 2016

---

7   Matthew 22: 37, 39

ACKNOWLEDGEMENTS

I have been trying to witness to a close friend recently that God is a 'God of Miracles'. Although like many she has a strong spiritual dimension to her life, she is extremely sceptical about the God of the Bible. So I told her about the story behind this book, and she has admitted that it has definitely made her think.

Firstly, there was the upfront gift from a dear Christian couple who believed so strongly in the project when I floated the idea with them, that they immediately sent me a cheque to cover the whole production cost – even before I had had a chance to bring anyone on-board. Then there was the second unsolicited gift that arrived through my door with a note saying that they felt the book needed to be sent to all members of General Synod, even though they had read only a very small part of it.

The time line to create this book ahead of the July 2016 General Synod was incredibly tight. Most publishers will admit they can, if occasion demands, fast track a book to market in six months – we were looking at trying to do this in just over eight weeks, and that was without a word of text having been written! The first challenge was to identify and approach twelve suitable contributors, and ask them – some of the busiest people I know – to produce their articles in just a few days. I am particularly grateful to Anthony Archer, Gavin Collins and David Ison for taking a lead in this area, and so encouraging others to come on-board swiftly. It is a mark of the importance with which all contributors held the project that they prioritised it the way they did, and I am very grateful to each one of them for doing so.

But the even greater miracle was the unexpected provision of two highly experienced professionals following an 'SOS' prayer for help. Both generously offered their services – without even having met me! They have walked with me every step of the way, holding my hand as I learnt the publishing ropes.

As such, I will forever be indebted to Simon Barrow, Director of Ekklesia, for contacting me 'out of the blue' and introducing himself. He rang the day I had my head in my hands wondering how on earth I was going to bring this book to market without any prior knowledge of publishing. Despite having his own tight deadlines,

Simon, along with Bob Carling, has overseen the full production schedule for this book within the most challenging of timeframes. You would not be reading this book without him, and I am deeply grateful!

Just twenty-four hours earlier Ruth McCurry, recently retired from SPCK, had also been in touch following a nudge from a friend and proved to be my other absolute God-send. She has been such wise and gentle counsel, enabling me to draw on her vast expertise on a full range of topics, and providing a sounding board whenever needed. She most definitely has one of the rarest gifts – that of the encourager, knowing just the right word to say at the right time to help spur me on my way.

I owe them both my deepest thanks – their support has meant more than they can ever know.

And then there are the range of materials required to make a book like this.

Firstly, the challenge of creating a cover that would say "evangelical" right from the start. I could only think of one artist I knew who could possibly help with this, Charlie Mackesy. Reconnecting with him has been one of the greatest joys of this book. I am incredibly grateful to him for letting us use his most moving and powerful of paintings: 'The Prodigal Daughter', which I first heard him talk about when we were both at St Paul's Onslow Square – an offshoot of Holy Trinity Brompton – nearly twenty years ago.

Similarly, it has been wonderful to get to know Yvonne Bell, who I managed to connect with just hours before she left for holiday and secured her permission to use her extraordinary piece: "Urban Mission".

At this point, it is critical that I also thank Bishop James Jones for letting me reproduce his foundational essay 'Making Space for Truth and Grace', which was originally published in 2007 by Darton, Longman and Todd in a book edited by the late Kenneth Stevenson, *A Fallible Church*. It was reading this essay during my walk through some of the darkest and most difficult days of my life that I first gained a glimmer of hope that there might actually be another way of engaging with scripture. I have so much to thank Bishop James for, not least his continued support and wise counsel through these past few years.

There are many others who have been integral to the success of this book, and I give thanks for each of them. There is one person in particular without whose support, encouragement and advice I know that I would not have had the courage to envisage this book in the form that it now is. David Ison has been a constant friend, adviser, encourager, supporter, and where needed challenger. He has made real the age old adage that 'two heads are better than one'. This book is so much the stronger for his input.

Finally, I am deeply grateful to you, the reader, for engaging with the book in the way that you are doing. We are all part of one large family, and independent of where we stand on this issue, we know that we are all loved equally by our wonderful Heavenly Father. I hope and pray that this book will be a blessing to you, and that you will use it to aid further discussion amongst your Christian friends.

Jayne Ozanne
Oxford
May 2016

LIST OF CONTRIBUTORS

Anthony Archer, Lay Reader

Anthony is a Reader in the Diocese of St Albans, is a member of the General Synod and the Dioceses Commission. He currently works as a management consultant, advising on senior appointments and governance. He has served the Church in various capacities, most notably as a former member of the Crown Nominations Commission. He has also served on the Councils of Wycliffe Hall, Oxford and Oak Hill College. His other current interests include being a Governor of the Royal Brompton & Harefield NHS Foundation Trust.

Rt Rev Paul Bayes, Bishop of Liverpool

A churchwarden's son, Paul was brought up in an evangelical church in the Diocese of Bradford. Having rejected the church as a teenager, he came to an adult faith whilst at university, and subsequently trained for ministry at Queens College Birmingham. He served as a parish priest, university chaplain and church planter for twenty-five years before beginning work for the Archbishops' Council as National Mission and Evangelism Adviser in 2004. He became Bishop of Hertford in 2010 and his election as Bishop of Liverpool was confirmed in July 2014.

Ven Gavin Collins, Archdeacon of the Meon

Gavin has been Archdeacon in the Portsmouth Diocese since September 2011, where he is also Diocesan Warden of Readers and Chair of the Portsmouth and Winchester Diocesan Academies Trust. Before this, Gavin spent 14 years in parish ministry in Cambridge and Chorleywood, and is a life-long convinced Evangelical, having served in his early years as Prayer Secretary of the Cambridge Christian Union and as a Methodist Local Preacher. He is committed to the mission and growth of the church, both at a local level and an international context, and has served as a trustee of Latin Link mission agency and of the London School of Theology.

Rt Rev Colin Fletcher OBE, Bishop of Dorchester

Colin found that his faith came first alive during his late teens at a Scripture Union House-party at Iwerne Minster. During his time at Oxford he gained an enormous amount from both the Christian Union and St Ebbe's, as well as from his College Chapel. After training at Wycliffe Hall he had a curacy at St Peter's Shipley, a large evangelical church in Bradford, and then at St Andrew's, Oxford, whilst also teaching at Wycliffe. During this time, he served as the Chairman of CYFA. In 1990s, after a period at Holy Trinity, Margate, he became Chaplain to George Carey. In 2000 he was made Area Bishop of Dorchester in the Oxford Diocese.

Rev Marcus Green, Rector

Author and musician Marcus Green is Rector of three rural parishes in North Oxfordshire. Originally from Lancashire, he was a worship leader at St Aldates' Oxford before training for ordination at Wycliffe Hall. He served a curacy under Stuart Bell at St Michael's Aberystwyth, before seeing St Catherine's Pontypridd grow into a thriving evangelical family church. Whilst working in parish ministry Marcus has also been involved in chaplaincies in the arts, tourism and the forces and has spoken (primarily on a Biblical understanding of the cross as worship) at Soul Survivor, New Wine Wales and Asbury Seminary, USA.

Very Rev Dr David Ison, Dean of St Paul's

Brought up in Brentwood, Essex, David went to university in Leicester and theological college in Nottingham, before a six-year curacy in Deptford, where he engaged in inner-city ministry and studied for a PhD in early church history. After three years of being a tutor at the Church Army training college, he became vicar of Potters Green, an outer housing estate in north Coventry. In 1993 he moved to Exeter to work in theological training, and from 1995 was a diocesan residentiary canon at Exeter Cathedral. In 2005 he became Dean of Bradford and then Dean of St Paul's in May 2012.

Rt Rev James Jones, former Bishop of Liverpool

James became Bishop of Hull in 1994 and Bishop of Liverpool in 1998. The emphasis of his ministry has been on both personal faith and social justice. He chaired the Hillsborough Independent Panel that led to fresh Inquests and to the new verdict of unlawful killing of the 96. He now serves as the Home Secretary's Adviser with a remit to work with the Families to review their experience of the justice system. He broadcasts regularly and in a recent Thought for the Day on BBC Radio 4 about diversity said, 'You can't be true to the Truth if you can't be true about yourself; and if God is the conceiver of love he's to be found wherever true love lies.'

Rev Cindy Kent, Broadcaster

Cindy was ordained in June 2008, following a long and successful career in the media. She is currently based in Minster on Sea. Many will know Cindy as the lead singer in The Settlers, and as one of the original co-founders the Arts Centre Group – a support group for Christians who are professionally engaged in the arts. She has held various Chaplaincy positions in London has been a and Trustee of The Christian Evidence Society. She still works occasionally as a freelance at Premier Christian Radio, where she was a presenter for nearly 20 years.

Rev Dr Hayley Matthews, Rector

Hayley is Rector of Holy Innocents' in Fallowfield, and also serves as Civilian Padré to 6MI Battalion and Honorary Chaplain of St Peter's House. She is a member of the National Executive for UNITE where she represents the

Faithworkers' Branch. She believes equality in all its forms is central to her priestly calling to justice and reconciliation, and so is a Trustee of both the LGBT Foundation and the William Temple Foundation. Working with the Centre for the Study of Christianity and Sexuality, she is involved in the 2016 Constructive Conversations for Theological Educators.

Jayne Ozanne, Writer and Speaker

Jayne is a leading gay evangelical who works to ensure full inclusion of all LGBTI Christians at every level of the Church. Having been a founding member of the Archbishops' Council for the Church of England (1999 – 2004) she is now once again a member of General Synod where she is involved in campaigning for a range of issues – particularly the poor and the marginalised. Following a career in international marketing and strategic management consultancy, she is now actively engaged through her writings and broadcasts in helping the Church develop and promote a positive Christian ethic towards the LGBTI community.

Ven David Newman, Archdeacon of Loughborough

David has been an Archdeacon in Leicester Diocese since 2009. Before that he served incumbencies as Team Rector of Emmanuel and St Mary's Loughborough and as Vicar of Ockbrook and Borrowash in Derby. At Emmanuel the church took the strapline 'Offering God's welcome, being changed by His love'. This sought to capture the balance of inclusive welcome and transforming discipleship initiated and resourced from God's generous grace. David chairs the Diocesan Board of Education, and enjoys both teaching and training. He enjoys walking in the Lakes and theatre, and performs his own one man show of Mark's gospel.

Rev David Runcorn, Author and Speaker

David is Associate DDO and Warden of Readers in Gloucester Diocese. His ministry has always included writing, spiritual direction, speaking, teaching and theological reflection. He has been a vicar, a chaplain at Lee Abbey, a diocesan Director of Ministry and has taught in theological colleges and courses including Trinity College, Bristol where he remains an Associate Lecturer. His special interests include spirituality, preaching and Pastoral Theology.

Rev Jody Stowell, Vicar

Jody is Vicar of St Michael and All Angels' Church Harrow Weald. She was on the leadership team of the Open Evangelical group, *Fulcrum,* between 2007 and 2013, where she wrote many key articles. Jody has been on the National Committee of WATCH (Women and the Church) since 2013. She sees working for gender justice as a key part of the Gospel, in order for all people to flourish in God's Kingdom. She has also written for various blogs including *Threads,* the Evangelical Alliance blog aimed at 20s/30s and *The Independent.*

FOREWORD

Challenging Times for Evangelicals

Colin Fletcher, Bishop of Dorchester

Teaching Ethics, as I did at Wycliffe Hall in the early 1980s, pre-sented very different challenges from those of today. Green issues were hardly on the agenda, and Global Warming was rarely, if ever, mentioned. Questions of economic justice were, of course, around, and nuclear disarmament was on many people's minds. Issues in Medical Ethics were becoming more complex as Scientific and Technological advances allowed us to do things that had only been speculated about previously. 'Rights' language was less prevalent though a woman's right to choose, and an embryo's right to life were recognised as being in tension with one another.

And what of Sexual Ethics, particularly in the context of teach-ing in an evangelical theological college? Most of the debates, if my memory serves me right (and others who I taught are welcome to challenge me on this) were focussed primarily on the question of the remarriage of divorcees (as most Evangelical Churches were not doing that then); sexual intercourse before marriage; and, then, very much in the third place, homosexuality. Although Wycliffe did have its own gay sub-culture this was scarcely acknowledged. Whilst other Colleges were known to have their own gay com-munities, it was tacitly assumed that the same was not true of the Evangelical ones. What is more that was to some extent a reflection of much of British Society in the early 1980s, the Gay Community, let alone the LGBTI one, was much less of an overt presence in the latter's midst. 'Coming Out' was an even more frightening prospect for a gay person than it is today. Life was so very different then.

Yet, even in Church circles, things were changing. The 1988 Lambeth Conference repeated the call of the 1978 Conference for the 'deep and dispassionate study of the question of homosexual-ity, which would take seriously both the teaching of Scripture and the results of Scientific and Medical research' (Resolution 64:1). The *Gloucester Report (Homosexual Relationships)* was published in 1979 whilst the *Osborne Report* ten years later was refused permission by the House of Bishops to be published in its name (See Issues Para 1.4). Elsewhere, both amongst our ecumenical partners, and in different parts of the Anglican Communion, the debate was hotting up. Indeed, who will forget the so-called 'Higton Motion' which was passed by General Synod in November 1987 by an overwhelming majority (403 to 8)?

By the mid-1990s I was working as Chaplain to Archbishop George Carey and so was heavily involved in the 1998 Lambeth Conference. I remember very vividly the passion of the debate about what became Resolution 1:10 and the joy of some, and the pain of others, who were there. In 2000 I became Bishop of Dorchester and I served on the Design Group for the Lambeth Conference of 2008 where questions of sexuality were never far away from the challenging task of shaping the agenda.

In the meantime, in the Church of England at any rate, *Issues in Human Sexuality – A Statement by the House of Bishops* (published in December 1991) had become a key document. Today all would-be ordinands are required to have discussed it with their Diocesan Director of Ordinands and to have expressed that they are content to live within its guidelines prior to going to a Bishop's Advisory Panel.

Yet, if in the Church of England and the Anglican Communion we were discovering that we needed to address some of these issues with a greater degree of urgency, our challenge was that British Society was changing its beliefs even more rapidly. Over the past few years Civil Partnerships have become an accepted part of life as, increasingly, have same-sex marriages.

As a result, over the past 15 years as a bishop I have been asked by a growing number of my clergy colleagues if they can offer something more substantial than a few private prayers to mark the public affirmation by a same-sex couple of their commitment to one another. Likewise, I have noticed that some clergy are increasingly feeling able to be more open about their own same-sex partnerships, whether or not these have been formalised in a civil partnership or even in marriage. Pastorally and missionally too whilst *Issues* in 1991 may have been able to say with some degree of credibility that *'...given the present understanding of such '(sexually active homophile)' partnerships in the Church as a whole, it is unrealistic to suppose that these clergy in most parishes be accepted as examples to the whole flock as distinct from the homophiles within it' (Issues 5:16)* that basis for its reasoning is looking increasingly questionable today. Recent surveys among Church members strongly indicate that attitudes that were there in a previous generation have now changed.

And what of my fellow Evangelicals? What of the challenges for us? On one level it is very good that there are now Evangelicals who are willing to acknowledge that they are gay. Indeed, I want to record my particular thanks to people like Vaughan Roberts, Ed Shaw and Sam Allberry who have had the courage to both talk openly about their same-sex attraction and to write about it. However, and very importantly, alongside them are other gay Evangelicals, including a number of my colleagues here in Oxfordshire, who have studied the Bible and have reached different conclusions about what a holy lifestyle might, or does, mean for them. The same differences in scriptural understanding are, of course, present in the straight evangelical community as well.

Clearly we are in difficult territory here but my plea in contributing to this book of essays is that we should be unafraid to enter into this debate without excluding those who disagree with us.

I confess, for instance, that I get worried when I am told – as I was very recently – that this is a 'Gospel Issue'. I reflected on this afterwards and I concluded that what the speaker meant was that this would be some form of heresy and that they would leave the Church of England if we ever accepted same-sex blessings or marriages. Whilst I fully agreed with them that questions to do with humanity and sexuality are not merely matters of marginal interest or indifference, I do want to challenge the assertion that places them on an equal footing with the great credal truths of the Trinity or the humanity and divinity of Christ which we are called upon to proclaim afresh in each generation.

Pastorally too I am still saddened and shocked by Evangelical Churches who exclude gay men and women from holding office, even when they are un-partnered. Part of my learning curve has been to listen to their stories – lay and clergy alike – over recent years and to feel, at least to a small extent, the pain they experience. The damage being done to far too many good Christian people is immense.

But the crucial area to address, as ever, lies in Scripture and in its interpretation. Here the key questions are – is homosexual practice of the sort we know today in the context of stable, faithful, and permanent partnerships universally condemned in the Bible? And, even if we believe it is, does that mean that we have, of necessity, to refuse to share in the Mission of God with those who disagree with us?

There is not the space here to travel over the territory that was so recently addressed in Bishop Keith Sinclair's appendix to the Pilling Report, but what I have noticed just in the past two or three years is that there are an increasing number of Evangelicals who, like David Runcorn, are looking afresh at the Scriptures underpinning these debates, and particularly at the New Testament texts, and who are reaching different conclusions from the traditional interpretations of the past.

For instance, I have been fascinated and challenged by the exposition of Romans I which frames the chapter in terms of the sin of idolatry rather than on a focus on homosexual relationships in general. Or again by questions as to exactly what sorts of relationships Paul is condemning in 1 Corinthians and how they relate to what we encounter today.

Now, let me be clear, I am not personally arguing for a change in the definition of marriage as being between a man and a woman. I still think that it is a strong position to defend theologically. However, what I am pleading for is an openness amongst Evangelicals to discuss a range of differing beliefs to their own and to engage biblically with those who hold them without just writing such people off as 'revisionists' or (as described by a previous generation) 'woolly liberals'. The next stage – to acknowledge them as our fellow Evangelicals – may be very difficult indeed for some but is, I think, necessary, both for the health of the Body of Christ and for our mission to a world that is so much in need of the knowledge of his love.

In saying this I am, of course, only reflecting a key passage from *Issues* that, sadly, has not contributed as much as it should have done to the debates of the past 25 years.

Paragraphs 5:5 and 5:6 read as follows:

5.5 – 'Of Christian homophiles some are clear that the way they must follow to fulfil this calling is to witness to God's general will for human sexuality by a life of abstinence. In the power of the Holy Spirit and out of love for Christ they embrace the self-denial involved, gladly and trustfully opening themselves to the power of God's grace to order and fulfil their personalities within this way of life. This is a path of great faithfulness, travelled often under the weight of a very heavy cross. It is deserving of all praise and of the support of Church members through prayer, understanding and active friendship.

5.6 – At the same time there are others who are conscientiously convinced that this way of abstinence is not the best for them, and that they have more hope of growing in love for God and neighbour with the help of a loving and faithful homophile partnership, in intention lifelong, where mutual self-giving includes the physical expression of their attachment. In responding to this conviction it is important to bear in mind the historic tension in Christian ethical thinking between the God-given moral order and the freedom of the moral agent.

While insisting that conscience needs to be informed in the light of that order, Christian tradition also contains an emphasis on respect for free conscientious judgement where the individual has seriously weighed the issues involved. The homophile is only one in a range of such cases. Whilst unable, therefore, to commend the way of life just described as in itself as faithful a reflection of God's purposes in creation as the heterophile, we do not reject those who sincerely believe it is God's call to them. We stand alongside them in the fellowship of the Church, all alike dependent upon the undeserved grace of God. All those who seek to live their lives in Christ owe one another friendship and understanding. It is therefore important that in every congregation such homophiles should find fellow-Christians who will sensitively and naturally provide this for them. Indeed, if this is not done, any professions on the part of the Church that it is committed to openness and learning about the homophile situation can be no more than empty words.'

In other words, there was recognition even back in 1991 that Christians reach a variety of conclusions ethically and that therefore there should be space for all within our Church.

So in contributing to this book I hope that several things may stem from it.

First, that those Evangelicals whose studies of Scripture lead them to different conclusions from the traditional ones would be encouraged to find their voice in today's debates.

Secondly, and I realise that this is more problematical, that Evangelicals would accept each other as Evangelicals without resorting to the tactic of marginalising or excluding those they disagree with. As I say I recognise that this will be difficult to achieve but I think that it is extremely important for the health of Evangelicalism, both within the Church of England, and beyond it.

And thirdly, I hope that the damage still being done to members of the LGBTI communities would be lessened, if not eradicated, as they are welcomed, as we all should be, as fellow members of the Body of Christ. Such a welcome will, I am sure, also need to be accompanied by an appropriate element of apology for some of what has been done and said in the past if it is to be experienced as genuine and, in the same way, there will need to be immense graciousness expressed by those receiving it given the considerable cost it will involve. My conviction is that the sacrifices both will require will be worth it.

Finally, I am well aware that I have focussed this essay in the context of this book very much on evangelicalism within the Church of England. This is a world I owe a huge amount to, and know, and love. My hope is that others like me, and like the other contributors to this book, will continue to wrestle with these challenges and that God's Church, and God's Mission, will emerge all the stronger as a result.

Chapter 1

Open Table, Open Mind

Paul Bayes, Bishop of Liverpool

Cornelius and the Conversion of Peter

*'And [Peter] said to them, "You yourselves know that it is unlawful
for a Jew to associate with or to visit a Gentile; but God has shown
me that I should not call anyone profane or unclean."'*[1]

For the whole of my ministry I have sought to be a wise evangelist;
to find good ways of sharing the gospel of Jesus Christ within this
strange, complex, interesting culture. The love of God is unchang-
ing, and the culture is changing very quickly. In such a context,
what are we to do if we are to be authentic and to seek the Lord
Jesus where he said he would be? In my experience, always, conversion has begun and still begins by listening to those on the edge.
This is true for the conversion of non-Christians, and it is true for
the conversion of bishops.

It was with Professor Walter Hollenweger, the Swiss Reformed
pastor and world authority on the history of Pentecostalism, that I
learned the theology of mission. For Hollenweger the story of Peter
and Cornelius as told in Acts 10 was a formative text. He would say:
'Here we read of the conversion of Cornelius; but surely we also
read of the conversion of Peter'.

Peter's vision of the sheet full of unclean creatures,[2] and of the
voice of God declaring God's creation clean, radically changes him.
Changed as he is, he opens himself to an encounter with Cornelius
and his friends that changes him further, as he sees the work of
the Spirit evident in them. This brings him into trouble with the
Church.[3] Let Hollenweger take up the story:

---

1   Acts 10:28 (all Scriptural references are to the NRSV)
2   Acts 10:11ff
3   Acts 11:2,3

'When frontiers are crossed, when new dimensions of faith are discovered – above all when this is in contradiction to hitherto dearly-held principles – it seems that quarrel in the Church is inevitable. That was already the case in the original Christian community. Quarrel belongs to the Church. That does not necessarily mean that those who quarrel have to reproach each other with dishonest motives. According to Luke's text the apostles allowed Peter to present his story. And now a very remarkable thing happens. They are won over by the facts (emphasis added) – not by evidence from Scripture...'[4]

The response of the Jerusalem community to Peter's story, which is presented by him without any reference to scriptural exegesis, is unequivocal: *'When they heard this, they were silenced. And they praised God, saying, "Then God has given even to the Gentiles the repentance that leads to life".'[5]* Hollenweger goes on:

'Where did this astonishing confidence come from? "There can only be one answer" writes Lesslie Newbigin in discussing the commissioning of the missionaries from Antioch, "It is because they are convinced that these new Christians have received the Spirit". I have mentioned only a few of the difficulties in this remarkable story. However critically one might comment on it, no one can disregard the fact that it is part of the Bible... The disturbing fact in this story is just this, that an apostle who was called to be a rock in the Church learns something in the course of his evangelism which he had not known before. But, tell me, is evangelism any different today?'[6]

Extending the Table

In my installation sermon as Bishop of Liverpool I spoke of the table of the champion of the poor, Jesus Christ, and of my belief that Jesus wanted that table to be extended down every street and into every home so that He might sit beside all who want to sit there.[7] I did not know, when I wrote this sermon, of the existence of Open

---

4   Walter Hollenweger, *Evangelism Today: Good News or Bone of Contention?* (Christian Journals Ltd, Belfast, 1976) p.15
5   Acts 11:18
6   Walter Hollenweger, *Evangelism Today: Good News or Bone of Contention?* pp. 16–17
7   For the full text see http://bit.ly/1V61eYk

Table, which is an LGBTI congregation in the city of Liverpool. But I did know, and you too will know because it has been said repeatedly across the Church, that if we are to resolve our conversations around same-sex issues, then among other things we must listen closely and carefully to the experience of LGBTI people and among them to the experience of LGBTI Christians.

Listening closely and carefully to people is in itself a spiritual discipline. Evangelists in particular need to learn it. Too often it seems easier to speak, and if necessary to shout, until people say that they agree with me. Without careful listening we're left with raw contention. And goodness knows, we are used to that. As Walter Hollenweger remarks above: 'quarrel belongs to the Church'. But as an evangelist, I know that if I listen closely and carefully to people, then I will draw close to the moment of conversion – not only theirs but also mine. This was Peter's experience with Cornelius.

In today's England it's not difficult to listen to the life experience of LGBTI people. My own extended family includes a number of partnerships and a fair number of children; the children of opposite-sex marriages, the children of a civil partnership, the children of a same-sex marriage. All these children seem to play well together, though the parents of some of them have had difficulty in finding a welcome in the Church of Jesus Christ. But when the welcome has been extended, it has been warmly received, and conversion and discipleship have resulted. It was with this experience among others in my heart that I attended Open Table.

In the Appendix you will read a sketch of the history of Open Table, written by those who lead it. When I visited this congregation on its seventh birthday to celebrate the Holy Eucharist with them, I encountered in them the face of the Christ of the poor. The quality of this fresh expression of the Church struck me so forcefully that I was moved to give them a gift. It is reproduced overleaf.[8]

This icon was written (as the Orthodox say) by a woman who was a member of one of the congregations which I served as a parish priest. It portrays the Lord Jesus Christ among the broken poor. When I gave it to the Open Table congregation, I sought to make clear to them that it was not their sexual orientation that I saw as brokenness. I said that for many of their friends who lived in this

---

8   Icon: 'Urban Mission' by Yvonne Bell. http://christian-art.vpweb.co.uk/

TO BIND UP HEARTS THAT ARE BROKEN

TO BRING GOOD NEWS TO THE POOR

TO PROCLAIM LIBERTY TO CAPTIVES

AND COMFORT THOSE WHO MOURN

society at risk and in fear, they themselves were the face of Christ shining. The fact is that Open Table's Christians like so many LGBTI people, have been bruised and broken by our society's response to who they are. The harsh fact is that the Church has played, and still plays, no small part in this bruising and breaking. I therefore felt, and still feel, the obligation to repent on behalf of my sisters and brothers. I wanted to express my sorrow to this small and faithful congregation for the way in which Christians had treated them. I also wanted to express my thanks to them for continuing to minister and evangelise in the name of Jesus Christ despite all this.

Listen. In the midst of Liverpool (and of course this is not unique to Liverpool) is a congregation of over forty LGBTI men and women, seeking to follow Jesus Christ out of the truth of who they are. Many of them have suffered street violence for their sexual orientation, and some of them continue to do so. In the midst of this pain, they have expressed the love of Jesus Christ not only to the LGBTI community but also to the wider Church. And in my attempts to give close attention to this experience, I have myself been profoundly changed.

The Church conforms itself to Jesus Christ when it sees the face of Jesus Christ. In a famous and compelling passage, Pope Francis has said: 'I prefer a Church which is bruised, hurting and dirty because it has been out on the streets, rather than a Church which is unhealthy from being confined and from clinging to its own security.'[9] Among the many privileges of my life as Bishop of Liverpool is the opportunity to meet Christians who are poor, and who from their poverty are sharing extraordinary spiritual riches. This is true for example of our inner urban congregations, and in the same way it is true of Open Table. This group of people has been marginalised and frequently despised, and yet they remain faithful, supporting not only one another but also those in the wider world who suffer the same pains of exclusion and hurt.

The experience of Open Table is not the only experience of gay Christians in Liverpool. I have spoken here with gay people who feel called in their own lives to observe, in full, the traditional teachings of the Church and to conform their own behaviour to these teachings. 'This is a path of great faithfulness, travelled often under the weight of a very heavy cross.'[10] I respect it, as I respect any freely-accepted embracing of celibacy by those, across all the long history of the Church, who have been called to it. But I must also respect the experience of those who feel, after a great deal of prayer and reflection, that their sexuality is a gift from God, to be celebrated as any gift is celebrated. I respect this all the more if it exists in the context of a commitment as Christian disciples to bring the love of Christ to the world and to the broken poor.

How wholeheartedly will we respond to the frequently repeated injunction to listen to the experience of LGBTI people? In my own case, as I listen to that experience across the Diocese, how am I also to listen to the love of God as the Christians of Open Table receive and share it, and as those like them in every diocese and in

---

9   Apostolic Exhortation *Evangelii Gaudium* of the Holy Father Francis (2013) para 49
10   *Issues in Human Sexuality* (Church House Publishing, London, 1991) para 5.5

every city receive and share love? And what then must we do? It is with these questions that I continue to wrestle as a pastor and as a Bishop. It is these questions, heard in the light of the experience of Peter in the Scripture, which God addresses to me. Indeed, it is because of these questions that I have come to believe that we need to change the Church – to make room and to extend the table. How we might do so is the matter for our ongoing conversation. But that we should do so is evident to me.

To paraphrase Dr Martin Luther King, 'the arc of Scripture is long, but it bends towards justice'. That was Peter's experience, and it is proving to be mine.

Chapter 2

An Ordinary Bloke

Marcus Green, Rector of Steeple Aston

In the Spring of 2003 I was invited to appear on the BBC TV show *The Weakest Link*.

A mate of mine had seen an ad asking for people to audition for the show, and he and I both applied. Really, I did it just to annoy him. He was much brighter than me, and better at that sort of thing. Of course, he never heard back – whereas here was I, getting ready to travel to London to record my appearance.

Perfect.

Except … a couple of mornings before the recording, I was walking the dog and it occurred to me that Anne Robinson was likely to ask if I was gay. I was an unmarried vicar, and it was a standard question she threw out in the typical, mean, acerbic manner of the character she adopted to present the show.

Of course, I *am* gay. But at the time almost no-one knew.

As I thought about this, the fun of going to London to be on the quiz became completely overshadowed by the fear of what I would do if she asked this simple question.

I mean – my family didn't know. My parish didn't know. I wasn't about to come out on national TV. I'd spent years hiding in plain sight so I could operate as an Evangelical in ministry and not come under suspicion over this. In 2003, attitudes towards gay people hadn't quite yet become the supreme measure of orthodoxy, but it was always simplest to answer the question, 'Are you married?' with a 'Not yet!' in order to deflect attention. And I was still young enough to get away with that answer.

But what would I do if I was asked a straight (ahem) question on TV? I couldn't lie. So I couldn't say, 'No'.

I walked through the woods that morning getting increasingly anxious about a question I might never face. I got home and sat there, silent and still, frightened of what might happen. I spent a whole day thinking through a hundred different options.

7

≥▲

My story is the story of the ordinary bloke who gets caught up in life. I'm no one. Most of you reading this have (quite rightly) never heard of me. Like many others, I went to University and was involved in the CU (elected to the Exec, even). I was then on the staff at St Aldates, Oxford, leading worship for a while. I took a break for six months, travelling around (mostly) Bible-Belt America, before returning to England and training for ordination at Wycliffe Hall. A thoroughly typical evangelical pedigree.

When I was asked to be on the CU Exec I was asked if I was gay. I did lie that time. In my defence, I was twenty and desperate to be straight. It was an aspirational answer. It was a sinful question.

I just wanted to serve Jesus. Why should who I fancy make any difference to that?

I knew I was gay in my mid-teens. I knew I was gay at University. I knew I was gay at Wycliffe – and in those three years had a hell of a time as God, in his infinite kindness, made me really face up to the truth of it. Wycliffe was not an easy place to face up to that truth, and I sort of half got there. I'd edge towards seeing it, accepting it, and then hear a fellow student make some off-colour joke and run away from myself all over again. Not their fault – how could they know – and yet God in his mercy wouldn't let me off the hook. At the end of my time there, Dick France, the then principal at Wycliffe (whom many will remember personally, and far more will know of through his writings) called me into his study for stern words. I had failed to do all sorts of things I should have done, I had missed events and courses, he was not going to commend me for ordination.

In my shock, I knew I had the choice to be silent and watch my life disappear; or I could risk being honest with Dick and see what that did. So I told him. I told him – I've been coming to terms with being gay, and that's why I've missed things and been absent and been erratic, because I've been through emotional torment. No excuse, I'm really sorry, but there it is.

Dick became one of my heroes and a life-long friend that day. I was no one. Just another student there amongst so many he saw go through that place – and I was fortunate to study alongside some genuinely amazing people. I don't think many, however, can have experienced the pastoral care and personal Bible study that I had with Dick that day, over the weeks that followed, through ordination and in the years after as I went from curate to incumbent, and as I even had my first book published.

ॐ

All I wanted to do was serve Jesus. Tell people about Jesus. Lead folk to Jesus in worship, teach them about Jesus from the Scriptures. My desires were no different from anyone else's. Only, as time passed and I worked through my first incumbency, this became suddenly really hard.

We changed. We – Anglicans, especially Evangelicals – we changed. It became hard to hide in plain sight. It became hard to be a gay man and an Evangelical. I used to go to leaders' meetings in the various strands we have, our support networks and conferences, and suddenly orthodoxy started to include Jesus and 'traditional' views on sexuality. We changed. I had to develop this ability to appear to smile and agree with things I did not agree with, without actually agreeing. But I had to appear to do so. It mattered. It didn't when I was first ordained. It did now.

I'd sit there thinking – do you see what I spend my life doing? I'm just like you! I work twelve hours a day (at least) growing a church. I don't have hundreds of people – that's not my reality. But I see some folk transformed by the Spirit. I see some lives turned around. I see the love of Jesus touching people who had no idea. I see a town centre church that was teetering towards closure now filled with a life whose identifying marks are worship, evangelism and compassion.

And still you're asking me why I'm not married?

Does it matter?

The joke was: on the one hand, I was feeling the burn of suspicion from the new orthodoxy of my evangelical friends; and on the other, within my parish one bloke thought I was after his wife, and my mother was every other month trying to marry me off to some new female parishioner...

Eventually I am afraid it all became too much for me. I took a break from ministry because I needed to do again what I had done at Wycliffe. I needed to come to terms with who I was. I needed to stop hiding in plain sight. I needed to be honest. I needed not to have a clever answer about my sexuality; I needed to be able to give a simple one.

And I couldn't go through all that and still grow a church.

&

I started by going to Kentucky for a month.

This isn't the obvious place for someone working through sexuality issues to find peace... But I wasn't looking to find peace. I was looking to find Jesus. A friend of mine was working at an evangelical seminary there and offered me space, and it seemed like a good option.

Indeed, it was a very good option.

I had time with a remarkable Christian psychotherapist who helped me see that over the years I had simply accepted that as a gay man I was a second class Christian. Indeed, a second class human being. Knowing the truth does set you free; sometimes it takes someone else to help you see the truth about yourself. I had that gift in Kentucky, and the freedom that followed was immense. There are no second class members of God's kingdom. I know the Scriptures well enough to know this intellectually. But I had to be helped to see I'd taken on a terrible attitude and let it rule my life. And then I had to make sense of my life on the other side of that truth.

God blessed me: I had good friends around me, Bible scholars, folk who held differing views on sexuality but equally high views on Scripture with whom I could talk and work through the things I was learning about myself.

I learned this: I was deeply, deeply broken. All that time I had spent hiding in plain sight, I was not hidden – I was broken. Hiding? I was pretending. I may have fooled others; I mostly deceived myself. I am not straight. That normality is strange to me, and it cripples me. It is a lie. It does not fit. It damages me.

I had to learn how to be truly me, faithfully, worshipfully, Christ-centredly and honestly me.

And before I could serve people and point them to Jesus, I had to stop; spend time with Jesus; and discover who the honest, not-hiding, gay me was with him.

2&

I said that this is the story of an ordinary bloke who gets caught up in life. So it is. Life at this point was a whirlwind, but fortunately for me we Anglicans have ways of dealing with whirlwinds. I called my archdeacon.

I received exemplary care from my archdeacon, from my archbishop and from the bishop of the diocese I subsequently moved to. The archdeacon and archbishop in the diocese where I was an incumbent had no idea – absolutely no idea – what I'd been going through. It was a diocese without many Evangelicals, and the shock on their faces when I opened up to them was not well hidden! But the compassion, care and ongoing protection they offered were all superb. Our Anglican systems can be fantastic; I am a big fan.

It became clear to me I had to stop being an incumbent. My days in ministry were numbered as that stopping-to-spend-time-with-Jesus became ever more pressing. There we go; being single has its advantages when you have no-one else depending on you. There is a freedom to act which I understand others cannot so easily pursue. My archbishop tried to dissuade me at first, and then sought to help in whatever way I needed, ultimately in helping make contact with the bishop in the diocese I moved to as I found secular employment.

Emails, phone calls, visits – my archdeacon sometimes just sat there with me talking about music or films or anything just to spend a little time with me and show that I was not alone when I was feeling very alone. There were days I was incredibly angry with the Church for the twists in the journey I was experiencing; but it was the Church, the people of God, that believed in me when I stopped believing in myself, and it was the Church that sheltered me through the storm, even if all I could see was the way the wind kept blowing outside and in.

ે

Cut me, I bleed evangelical. It's my background, my foreground, my whole life in ministry. I love the Scriptures. I can't take on a position on anything – still less something that matters to me personally – unless I am happy that I have a Biblical viewpoint on it. I had good tutors. They taught me well.

When I was on the CU Exec, we would go to UCCF[11] training days. We were taught how to recognise a 'false gospel'. The true gospel gives us Jesus; a false gospel is always 'Jesus and...' This is why I am sure that many of my friends on the more conservative side of our sexuality debates don't – can't – mean everything that gets said in the heat of the moment. We come from the same place. That orthodoxy should be 'Jesus and traditional sexuality' is clearly a false gospel, and my conservative friends no more believe in any false gospel than I do. We have all been taught well – even if we all occasionally forget ourselves.

So as I worked my way through how to reconcile being gay with being Christian, Evangelical, and (hopefully again one day) a minister of the gospel, I worked my way through Scriptures. I'm not going to go into detail here as to how I read St Paul in Romans and what I found there. I'm trying to get something published, and if I've any luck then one day you might brush up against that by accident somewhere else. I'm not going to give you my workout of why the Jew/Gentile debate is the definitive word on there being no second class Christians, and how that works as a direct correlation for these debates of ours.

I am, and given my story it should come as no surprise, going to take for a moment the more personal Biblical touch. A 'people' story.

It is a common-place that there is nothing in the Gospels about homosexuality. But there is everything about how Jesus deals with people. I am not an issue, apologies, I am a person, and so actually I find an awful lot in the Gospels that hits the spot directly for me.

In the two years I spent away from full-time ministry, I worked at a University. I was also attached to a parish, and was well looked

---

11   Universities and Colleges Christian Fellowships – now UCCF: The Christian Unions

after both by the vicar there, and (as I've mentioned) the local bishop – who gave me far more time and care than I had any right to expect.

Having preached as an incumbent something like four times a week for eleven years, I didn't preach at all for a year. My second or third sermon after that time came at the end of October 2012, and the passage I preached on was from the end of Mark 10.

My work at the University involved me taking a journey with the director of our art gallery. We were going to view some works that might be displayed at the University, and we travelled by train together. We discussed all sorts of things on the journey. The gallery director told me of her plans for the weekend, and asked me mine. I told her I was preaching at church. She was fascinated – she was Jewish and asked me all sorts of questions. So I gave her an outline of my sermon.

And as I did, I was for a moment caught up in my complete enthusiasm for the text and its power and the story and how it has the ability to change lives. I saw something in my colleague's eyes as I spoke. And I realised that – much as I enjoyed my life and work at the University – my heart was elsewhere. Where you heart is, there your treasure is also.

Then I preached on the Sunday.

I spoke of blind Bartimaeus calling out to Jesus, 'Son of David, have mercy on me!' This is Mark's final story before Jesus enters Jerusalem. Throughout Mark's Gospel, Jesus has kept who he is quiet, and now as they leave Jericho others are telling the blind man to be quiet, but Jesus wants him to speak up. Then there is the wonderful question as Jesus asks, 'What do you want me to do for you?' and the text gloriously adds, 'The blind man said, "Rabbi, I want to see".'

Sometimes salvation is the healing of things that have been wrong for a long time.

Jesus is the first Son of David, the first king in David's line, for hundreds of years to be acclaimed as king in Jerusalem. The last king in David's line was Zedekiah. He escaped Nebuchadnezzar's armies at Jerusalem, ran and was captured at the plains of Jericho. Jericho, where Jesus now is. There Zedekiah was forced to watch as his sons were killed, and then he himself was blinded.

Now Jesus hears a blind man cry out in Jericho and sees a chance to put right a 'long wrong'. Zedekiah's (and everyone's) redemption is coming.

My question to my congregation: so what is your 'long wrong'? And perhaps, to help you answer that, who are you – deep inside? Who do you see yourself as being? The blind man? Perhaps, perhaps not. The lonely person? The bereaved? The guilty? The sinned against? The poor? The thoughtless? The friendless? The ignored? The abused? Who?

When you have thought about who you are – then what do you want Jesus to do for you?

We preach to ourselves, of course. As I preached those words, I knew who I was. I am the gay man who is a minister of the gospel; and Lord, I want to serve. The thought went through my mind and I was hit by the love of Jesus; it was time to look for my next ministry post.

Mark 10.52: '"Go", said Jesus, "your faith has healed you." Immediately he received his sight and followed Jesus along the road.'

ॐ

The following encounter was broadcast in the first round of *The Weakest Link* on BBC1, during an afternoon in the autumn of 2003.

Anne: 'So Marcus:'

Marcus: 'Yes Anne?'

Anne: 'You're thirty-six, single and a vicar.'

Marcus: 'That's right.'

Anne: 'Are you gay?'

(Very audible intake of breath from the other contestants.)

Marcus: (pause, smile) 'Why Anne, are you checking to see if I'm available?'

It took me a day of thinking and being afraid to come up with those ten, relaxed 'off the cuff' words. That's no way to live, and I'm glad the world I knew then seems a very long way away.

Seriously, I'm no one. Just an ordinary bloke whose heart is to serve Jesus. That's why my story is here.

But please hear this: our churches are peppered with similar ordinary people who desperately need to be shown God's love so that they too may serve, and with all of us follow Jesus along the road.

❧

P.S.

In case you're wondering how I did on *The Weakest Link*...

I won!

Chapter 3

Principles and Prodigals

David Ison, Dean of St Pauls

Where Have I Come From?

Simon was leaving the church where I was vicar. He'd had enough of trying to be both an Evangelical Christian and a gay man, made more difficult by a very hard early life. Even though the church tried to welcome him, he couldn't get over his sense of rejection. So he was off to the big city to leave it all behind him. I assured him of our love and prayers for him, and that he'd find God there waiting for him. 'You b*******!', he said, 'leave me alone, I just want to be free.' There were tears in his eyes – and in mine. I often wonder what happened to him, and to the others like him I've known over the years.

Like many Evangelicals, I grew up as a Christian learning a doctrinal package of 'What the Bible says', with dire warnings about starting off on the slippery slope of questioning any aspect of it. While most of the time I could see how what I was told about the meaning of the Scriptures fitted with the texts, I was troubled by areas of inconsistency or issues which were ignored. These ranged from God-sanctioned genocide of Canaanites and prohibitions on usury to hostility among some Evangelicals to the work of the Holy Spirit in the charismatic movement. I began to discover the power of hearing Scripture speak in its own context as well as to mine, rather than finding in it what I expected to see. And then of course there was the vexed issue of sex.

It came home to me just how closely sexuality and Scripture are intertwined a few years after I was ordained. I was speaking at a seminar in St John's Nottingham theological college arguing why Artificial Insemination by Donor (AID) was unethical from a Christian standpoint, when Colin Buchanan, the then Principal, pointed out that my reasoning also implied that artificial contraception was wrong. I agreed, saying that I thought the Pope was right. Suddenly the atmosphere in the room changed, as an academic argument became intensely personal – I had questioned the assumptions of nearly all the married men in the room, who didn't have a pastoral issue with AID but had a big issue about having more children or less sex.

That taught me about the importance of letting Scripture interrogate my inherited assumptions and inherent self-interest, and also about how we can lazily assume that the way that those around us see things is the way that things really are. The Lambeth Conference of 1930 was the first Church body to allow that contraception within marriage might not be an evil thing. Did that decision make me and all of (official) Christendom throughout history wrong? Or was it the result of 'unbiblical' theology by the Anglican bishops? If it was because of the changing understanding of sexuality in society in the twentieth century, at what point does discontinuity between 'our' definition (whoever 'we' is) of what is sinful and the beliefs and practices of many Christian LGBTI people require us to reconsider our interpretation of Scripture as well as challenge our practice? It seems obvious that killing other people is wrong, but the Church has allowed capital punishment and war for centuries, contrary to the practice and words of Jesus. How does that therefore relate to what we tend to see as immutable matters of sexuality – into the interpretation of which are bound up all sorts of personal experiences, sorrows and sins?

Back in the 1970s whilst President of the Christian Union at Leicester University, I spoke in the Students' Union in support of a motion condemning discrimination against gay people, but abstained in the vote because I couldn't agree with the statement that gay relationships were as valid as straight ones. This summed up my approach for my first two decades in ministry: to love, care for and be alongside people whatever their sexuality or lack of it, while upholding core principles about the Christian understanding of sex. These include: that sex must be within commitment to one partner for life, and open to procreation, nurture and relationship-building; that polygamy (which is biblical) and divorce (which is biblical) are deviations from that norm; that Jesus tells us that there is no sex in heaven and that Paul would prefer no sex on earth, and that therefore singleness and celibacy are as valid as being partnered; and that all of us fall short of what is ideal and yet still receive God's mercy. God starts with us where we are and leads us on to be formed into the likeness of Christ, because God's love in Jesus Christ is inclusive and challenging for everyone.

Where am I Now?

Have I changed my mind about all that? No, not about the core principles. But challenged by the meeting of Jesus with a woman from Tyre who changed his presumption that the Good News was only for the House of Israel, I eventually listened to the experience of gay Christians themselves. I'm sorry to say that this was only after many years of making them fit my inherited narrative that they were in some way 'not proper Christians'.

This first happened at a conference I organised in Exeter before the debate in General Synod in July 1997 about the 1991 document *Issues in Human Sexuality*. At that conference I listened to the testimony of two gay men, thinking with my head that this was interesting, and wishing in my heart that I didn't have to hear what they were saying. To do so would mean that I would have to change the way I viewed my gay and lesbian brothers and sisters in Christ. More specifically, I would need to see them as people with things to teach me about how to interpret Scripture and how to live as a faithful Christian. Since then I've grown in appreciation for the living Christian faith and sacrificial ministries of many with whom I've worked and worshipped over the years.

I've also come to see the importance of LGBTI people having access to what I've termed 'the virtues of marriage'. That's not only for the well-being of society through promoting 'permanent, faithful, stable' and nurturing relationships, but also for the personal and spiritual growth of those engaged in committed self-giving love to another person which overflows in love and nurture into the wider community – just as we aspire to in heterosexual marriage.

That said, I haven't changed my mind on what the core principles around sexuality are, though I have changed my view about how some of them work out in practice. However, I don't think that the theory and the theology have yet been sufficiently integrated. So I'm not convinced that the theology of marriage can be separated from its roots of being between a man and a woman. I also think that the use of the adjective 'gay' or 'same-sex' in front of the word 'marriage' changes its meaning – as do adjectives such as 'Christian', 'Islamic' or 'secular'. It was recently reported that the artist Tracey Emin has 'married' a stone in her garden: what adjective would be appropriate for that, and what meaning does 'marriage' carry in that context?! I would therefore suggest that we have much work to do on what 'marriage' means in Christian understanding in a very different social context, and on what makes for consistent Christian ethics for LGBTI as well as heterosexual people.

Interpreting Scripture

How then do I understand 'what Scripture says' about homosexual practice and LGBTI people? It's important to state first that looking for 'what the Bible says' as if there is a single biblical perspective on everything isn't a valid way of reading Scripture. It assumes that Scripture has just one view, when the Bible is actually 66 books – which themselves may contain more than one perspective. Indeed, those books were written to share the Word of the Lord addressed to a whole variety of contexts, none of which are quite our own. A method of working which seeks to define 'what the Bible says' makes the interpreting authority the arbiter of truth, not the Bible itself. The Scriptures aren't an abstract statement of truth, but they are the stories of the experiences and understandings of God's people through time. They are stories which bear witness to the truth of God in Jesus Christ, who alone is the Word of God – the Word revealed in person.

I believe we therefore need a more radical approach, in the proper sense of that word. By that I mean, not sweeping away centuries of exegesis and experience, but rather doing the hard work of really engaging with it. The aim is to get to the roots (*radix*, hence 'radical') of what biblical texts mean. That's a corporate enterprise where we have to debate and work on Scripture in order to hear what God is saying to us. The Bible shows God's people seeking to interpret Scripture across time and culture inside the period in which Scripture was written, and we have to continue that process – as the history of contraception noted above illustrates. There will be core principles that we can agree on – such as loving God and our neighbour being central for Jesus, and so too for us – and there will also be applications of those principles that we may disagree on. We may even find ourselves following Jesus in arguing from first principles to set aside or go beyond some current interpretations of Scripture, such as with his view on divorce.

Part of the essence of this enterprise is to be as aware as possible of our own cultural context and our own blind spots. For this we need the alternative readings and experiences of our Christian sisters and brothers to challenge us, and about which we need not to be defensive.

For example, how culturally determined are Evangelical views on women formed in a patriarchal society? How consistent are such views with what we see in the stories of Jesus and read about in Paul? And how do they actually work out in practice? Or to take an alternative perspective, how far is the Holy Spirit speaking to the Church through social change, and how far is the Church in hock to the Spirit of the Age?

We have to work together respectfully on these things, rather than throwing self-justifying slogans at one another. We also have to do as Jesus advises us and 'look at the fruits', the outcomes, of what we believe. Put another way, what draws us and others into holiness, into the likeness of Christ, and what does not? What helps our journey, and what is a 'burden too heavy to bear' laid upon others?

Looking at the Texts

The first two chapters of Genesis set the scene for sexuality, where sexual differentiation is for procreation, companionship and right ordering of affections, in a context where God's people needed to increase in numbers to remain in existence in a dangerous world. As the tradition of celibacy indicates, the command to multiply is not the primary calling for the Christian Church – indeed human success in breeding and survival threatens the very viability of our planet. Some reconsideration of how we should now understand the Genesis perspective on marriage is necessary, as well as exploration on how far that should affect the underlying principles.

And that exploration continues. My views on the few explicit biblical texts on 'homosexual practice' (which is an anomalous term for biblical times) are open not closed – particularly as we continue to engage with the dialogue between texts and contexts.

In the Old Testament, the story of Sodom in Genesis 19 is about abuse of powerless strangers, hardly mitigated by Lot 'the righteous man' (2 Peter 2.8) offering his daughters to be raped instead. The prohibitions on 'lying with a male as with a woman' in Leviticus

18.22 and 20.13 are in the context of surrounding pagan societies where sex was used in idolatrous ritual practices. They form part of instructions about ritual cleanness which include, not only aspects of sexuality such as incest and sexual activity during menstruation (and how many churches have a position on this?), but also many other things, some of which Christians still uphold, but many of which are no longer observed – such as not eating blood, leaving harvest gleanings, not mixing clothing fibres and not having tattoos.

These texts in the Torah have to be assessed for their ongoing relevance to Christian faith on grounds other than whether or not they offend against ritual purity, given that Christians no longer recognise the ritual law as authoritative in itself. 'All things are lawful, but not all things are beneficial' says Paul (1 Corinthians 10.23), and it's on Christian grounds that we need to discriminate as to what this means.

What of the New Testament texts? The appropriate translations for *malakoi* ('softies') and *arsenokoitai* ('men-liers') in the lists of sinners in 1 Corinthians 6:9–10 and 1 Timothy 1:10 are disputed. That said, the context is a fairly conventional list of how the law names idolatrous and godless behaviour – which those two words refer to – in order to lead to salvation in Christ, analogous to the list in 1 Corinthians 5.9–11 of how Christians can behave in ways faithless to God.

The argument in Romans 1.16ff is similar: Paul addresses Jews and Greeks on how they are sinners in need of redemption, by beginning with a description familiar to Jews of moral degeneracy caused by Gentile idolatry, which leads not only to 'unnatural' sexual conduct but also to deliberately rebellious wickedness. He then goes on in chapter 2 to implicate Jews too in such behaviour, with all in need of salvation in Christ.

Paul's use of the concept of 'natural' comes out of in his particular contextual understanding of what natural means – concepts we and others may not share. Is long hair for men, or short hair for women, or women speaking in church (see 1 Corinthians 11 and 14) also 'unnatural' in different cultural contexts of education, fashion and religious practice? The early Church was very exercised about Greek cultural practices of older men corrupting boys, and the Pauline texts also need to be read against that background of concern about power and abuse.

The question is not only what these texts mean in their own context, but also how they apply in a different context. How can texts about idolatrous behaviour and self-gratification apply straightforwardly to a faithful, equal and loving same-sex relationship between Christians?

Where Might We Go?

The deeper issues of principle which I've already alluded to are part of this discussion. One of the fundamental questions is what actually constitutes sinful behaviour in relation to sexuality. In my view, this has to be seen in context – in working out what, in a given culture, constitutes disordered or promiscuous sexual behaviour which is destructive and sinful, whether it's culturally acceptable or not. The Church has been doing that working out for centuries, not only with contraception, but with changes in the understanding of marriage and divorce (in some cultures cousin marriage is allowed, for example, in others it is seen as incest). The Church needs to do the same for LGBTI ethics. We can't simply read off verses from the Scriptures as if they can be free from cultural contexts and assumptions, or transfer morality uncritically from one historical or contemporary culture to another. Doing so does not make an adequate argument for why faithful life-long committed same-sex partnership should not be an option for faithful Christian people.

The challenge facing us is to work through how we can move from where we are as a Church to a more truthful and consistent place, because the fruits of our current views and practices have too often been destructive. LGBTI people have felt unwanted and been excluded from churches or sadly even hounded into breakdowns or worse. There is a lack of honesty about people's sexuality and situations. There is inconsistency between public and private policy which corrupts church life and brings the Gospel into disrepute. There are too many who, like the Simon I knew, want to have faith but can't cope with the hypocrisies of the Church.

There are no easy answers to what it means to love and serve God and our neighbour, whatever our approach to sexuality. However, I firmly believe that discussion, argument, disagreement, encounter and change will be an integral part of our journey together, as we enter more deeply into the mystery of the inclusive and challenging love of God in Jesus Christ our Lord.

Chapter 4

A Lifetime of Learning

Anthony Archer, Lay Reader

It is often assumed that Evangelicals who are seen to have changed their mind on the issue of homosexuality must have been strongly influenced by the experience of a close family member or friend. Like many, I have gay friends, however while there have been instances of gay and lesbian members of my family in the past, to my knowledge there are none currently. That said, all my three godparents were probably gay or lesbian, which may be quite an unusual fact given my generation!

Early Life

My great uncle was the first gay man that I got to know. A wonderful eccentric, raconteur and a great host, he lived with his partner for many years until the latter's death, in the decades when open relationships were comparatively rare, and indeed in their early years together male homosexual acts were illegal. I recall my father briefing me on him in a rather endearing way. Of course I didn't need the parental education! Rather less spoken about was the experience of my mother's sister, a committed Christian, whose life was tragically shortened by multiple sclerosis. She had a constant friend and companion. I never asked my parents about their relationship, but it seemed clear to me that it was a close one and marked by covenant faithfulness. A sadder example was my third godparent, whose life was badly scarred at the hands of the Japanese in World War II. A public figure, with a profound faith, he had eventually fallen on hard times financially and his marriage had collapsed. I was pleased to learn that some years later he found friendship with another man.

Secular Encounters

My business career, unsurprisingly, has been marked by working together with gay and lesbian colleagues. In most cases I had no knowledge of their sexuality, both one or two that I personally recruited for my team, and those I assisted clients to recruit. I was articled to a gay man in the 1970s; he was an excellent role model and his private life had no bearing on me and I don't recall colleagues in the firm ever commenting.

It is only as I recall these people in my early life and career that I wonder what influence they may have had on my thinking and views on sexuality. The fact that they were gay played almost no part in how I saw them and regarded them. And yet, when I committed my life to Christ there was an unspoken understanding that I would automatically don the mantle of the Church's traditional teaching, whether I expressed my support for it or not.

Engaging with the Issue in Church

I can barely recall a sermon on sexuality, certainly not on the issue of homosexuality. The marriage covenant and the biblical injunction to faithfulness certainly featured in the biblical teaching I received, together with the implicit assumption that only heterosexual marriage is permitted. But I never found myself questioning it or really engaging with the practical outworking of that teaching, not least in the hearts and minds of a same-sex couple, until comparatively recently. Furthermore, I found other Evangelicals assuming that I must believe the traditional teaching or 'else I wouldn't be an Evangelical.' I therefore had to start to wrestle with the fact that the views I was assumed to hold had never actually been tested or truly owned by me.

Leading Alpha courses in the early days of the mid-1990s, the issue of homosexuality rarely if ever came up in small group discussions, while the question of pre-marital sex was far more common. However, the literature and course materials did present the Church's teaching on sex as being reserved for lifelong monogamous relationships between a man and a woman, with the consequent implications that all other forms of sexual activity outside marriage were prohibited.

Years ago in an Evangelical parish where I worshiped with my wife and family, a baby boy was presented for baptism by his mother and her lesbian partner. The mother had been a regular member of the congregation and her partner was an occasional visitor. As I reflect back, I now realise that we were not particularly welcoming (at least I know I wasn't) and it must therefore have taken some courage for her to attend. However, there were some more enlightened members of the congregation, including a saintly churchwarden who made it his business to befriend the mother. He generously took on the role of sponsor of the child at the baptism and beyond, which was a moving gesture that made me realise that whatever I may have thought about the Church's traditional teaching, what really mattered was showing love and grace to a fellow believer rather than standing in judgement over them.

Sex and the General Synod

My early years on the General Synod came well after Tony Higton's Private Member's Motion in November 1987 on the 'biblical standard' on sexual morality This was a motion that in the event was given much more moderate language by the amendment (often forgotten) of Michael Baughan, then Bishop of Chester. By then the House of Bishops had also published *Issues in Human Sexuality* (1991), a document that was to take on almost doctrinal status, despite not being debated in Synod until July 1997. This later debate is worth revisiting when looking at the issue today. Coming as it did before the 1998 Lambeth Conference, and all that that was to imply for the handling of the issue more widely in the Anglican Communion, George Carey said of the matter: 'It will not go away and it is no good pretending that opposition to, and acceptance of, homosexual practice are reconcilable opinions.'

I had put down a Private Member's Motion in 2004 on the subject of senior church appointments and the need for reform; it was debated in February 2005. Some Synod members seized on it and assumed it was a response to the nomination of Jeffrey John as Bishop of Reading. I assured commentators that that sorry affair was not the catalyst for the motion and although it was clearly passed and led to the influential report *Talent and Calling*, I was unable to shake off the suspicion that I was campaigning to continue to prevent the consecration of gay bishops, which I regret.

Towards a Change of Mind

How then did I come to express a view on homosexuality that challenges the Church's orthodox position? As the secular world came rightly to adopt a more inclusive stance towards all minorities, including those identifying as LGBTI, I realised (somewhat slowly to my shame) that the position of the LGBTI Christian community was, in contrast, acutely difficult. Until I started to get to know some gay and lesbian Christians, I had almost no idea of the hostility towards them and the sheer difficulty, indeed impossibility for some, of finding a place of worship that was both inclusive and safe. Furthermore, I had no idea of the experience of LGBTI Christians discerning a call to priesthood and the complications that lay in store for them. Would the Church simply refuse to ordain them with all the implications that would have for God's call on their lives? Taken together with the fact that it had become clear to me that bishops had been ordaining gay priests since time immemorial and presumably also, since 1994, lesbian priests, I began to ponder the sheer hypocrisy of the Church's position. Call me naive perhaps, but I was a late developer in taking these issues on board.

Recent Reflections

Training to become a Reader in the Church of England has reminded me of the sources of faith and the threefold formulation 'Scripture, tradition and reason' – the characteristic Anglican model for perceiving revelation and understanding authority. But as an Evangelical, my starting point had to be Scripture. If I was to adopt any kind of affirming theology, however tentatively, how as an Evangelical could I do that without letting go of biblical authority? Could I afford to be labelled an ex-Evangelical? Would that matter? Actually I decided it mattered a lot. I needed to consider the texts that are regarded by conservatives as evidence that homosexuality is a sin regardless of the context. And I needed to consider the apparent severity of that sinfulness, the fact that some even believe it to be a salvation matter. It seemed a heavy duty task for a layman with my theological knowledge and yet something was nagging at me that the Church's current teaching seemed flawed. It just seemed too simple to argue that all homosexual acts are incompatible with Scripture.

Furthermore, such a stance focused on sexual acts to the complete exclusion of relationships. There seemed to be basic biblical principles at issue which, by being overlooked, allowed a purely binary approach to the problem.

Old Testament

The Old Testament fragments seemed the easier ones to put under the microscope. They clearly disproved of certain behaviour. The dark story of Sodom and Gomorrah in Genesis 19 is one of vicious abusive sexual acts perpetrated on outsiders for reasons of both lust and hatred. Homosexual gang rape used as a weapon against foreigners seems about as far removed as one can be from loving, committed same-sex relationships. Indeed, I started to realise that 'homosexuality' as we know it is a distinctly modern concept. There is no word in the Old Testament that translates into 'gay' or 'homosexual' and no corresponding concept of sexual orientation. I was helped in my understanding of the early history by Boswell. [12]

The story of Sodom is not an isolated episode. Judges 19 recounts the male Levite and his concubine travelling far from home. The Bible labels the actions by the men of Gibeah a horrific and vile crime, but to use them as the basis for a blanket condemnation of loving, faithful same-sex partnerships is a wholly erroneous judgement which the text cannot support. Likewise, many would assert that the Levitical prohibitions were purely a reference to the idolatrous practices of the pagan people who had previously inhabited the land. They were aimed as a warning to the Israelites against such behaviour.

New Testament

If issues of context were key to understanding the Old Testament references, they seemed even more material in dealing with the New Testament. Sodom and Gomorrah re-appear in Jude 7 where the emphasis is on the judgement of false teachers and the risks they face in forfeiting their first love through pursing unnatural lust. However, the most substantial reference to homosexuality appears in the widely debated Romans 1. Might this be the text that would stop me in my tracks and make me think again? My first observation was that I was completely unable to locate my LGBTI Christians friends anywhere in Paul's language. Homosexual relations appear as just one example of the reversal of the created order when humanity rejects God. The list includes covetousness, envy, boastfulness, and gossip. It would be a brave person who could not

---

12   John Boswell, *Christianity, Social Tolerance and Homosexuality* (University of Chicago Press, Chicago, 1980)

locate him or herself somewhere in this catalogue of sins at some point! And if the Jews thought they were in a superior position, then Paul disabuses them of that fanciful hope in Romans 2.

However, the inclusion of wrong sexual desires in verses 26–27 merits closer examination, as many Christians today would be very sensitive to that charge and would have to acknowledge that their lives also contain elements of sexual brokenness. What kind of sexual sin was Paul really driving at? As Boswell notes, only the most pressing moral questions are addressed by the authors of the New Testament. Gay relationships, whether sexual or not, would not have been cited as being a primary issue. Verse 26 is clearly a reference to heterosexual women exchanging natural intercourse for what would have been for them, unnatural. It makes no reference to lesbian relationships as we understand them today. Likewise, in verse 27, men – even more explicitly heterosexual men – are chastised for committing shameless acts with other men. The understanding of sexual orientation, even if known at the time, was not the focus of Paul's teaching. His concern was for men and women naturally attracted to each other yet abandoning that attraction for reasons of idolatry. The presenting issue was the idolatry not the homosexual acts, which were one of its consequences.

Likewise, Paul's arguments in 1 Corinthians[13] and 1 Timothy[14] need examination. The list of vices in the former passage bears similarities to Romans 1 and includes two Greek words *malakoi* and *arsenokoitai*, both the subject of extensive biblical scholarship, and usually understood as references to same-sex behaviour. But as Achtemeier[15] makes clear, in his singularly helpful book for Evangelicals, Paul is not offering the Corinthians any kind of nuanced or detailed moral analysis of particular sexual behaviour. His larger argument, expanded in chapters 5 and 6, was to challenge the 'anything goes' version of Christianity which was apparently prevalent at the time. This was evidently down to the fact that some Corinthian Christians had concluded that because they are forgiven through the grace of Christ, they were free to do anything they liked. As in the 1 Corinthians passage, 1 Timothy contains a vice list that is used as part of a larger argument.

---

13   1 Corinthians 6:9
14   1 Timothy 1:9–10
15   Mark Achtemeier, *The Bible's Yes to Same-Sex Marriage* (Westminster John Knox Press, Louisville, 2014)

Wider Biblical Principles

I then needed to consider the wider biblical principles and see how these chimed with the arguments over the presenting issue, which is actually same-sex marriage rather than homosexual acts. What might tradition and reason tell us? The judgement that all homosexual acts are sinful regardless of context seemed to pose a huge problem. While sins of adultery and fornication (and more common sins of a non-sexual type) can be dealt with by believers through their repentance and Christ's forgiveness, 'for I will forgive their iniquity, and remember their sin no more',[16] this kind of 'sin' appeared to be in a different category.

The stark binary argument to be applied was that repentance for this kind of 'sin' would have to carry the burden of forgoing any kind of intimacy and covenant relationship for life. Not for same-sex believers the privilege and joy of having a 'companion'. It seemed to defy any kind of 'moral logic', a whole approach to the issue helpfully explored by Brownson.[17] The more I have got to know and count as friends Christians who identify as LGBTI the more I have been convinced that their sexual orientation is the way God created them. Moreover, He did not do it to make an example of them or to compel them to a life of forced abstinence.

Why would a loving God want to withhold His blessing from one particular group of people? What conceivable harm is done by two people of the same sex entering into a relationship which they hope and pray will be lasting, covenanted and monogamous, in the same way as a couple of the opposite sex? The arguments lead into an understanding of natural law, marriage and the purpose of sex, all helpfully explored by John.[18]

My detractors will argue that I am simply being swayed by experience as a result of which I have had to conclude that the Bible does not contradict what I have come to believe through that experience. Well, I have certainly addressed the latter and do conclude that the Bible does not include a blanket prohibition, with the associated penalty of the denial of salvation, on homosexual acts. In much the

---

16   Jeremiah 31:34b
17   James V. Brownson, *Bible, Gender and Sexuality* (Eerdmans, Grand Rapids, Michigan, 2013)
18   Jeffrey John, *Permanent, Faithful, Stable* (Darton, Longman and Todd, London, 2012, new edn)

same way as Scripture has been the subject of intense debate over such issues as slavery and the place of women, the presenting issue today – and one that is capable of tearing the Church apart and imperilling its mission – is same-sex marriage.

Looking Ahead

So is there a way forward? *The House of Bishops Working Group on Human Sexuality* (Pilling) remains the current reference document for the Church of England, from which the model for the Shared Conversations was developed. *Pilling* was nuanced in many ways but at least committed the Church to profound reflection on the interpretation and application of Scripture. It was clear on homophobia, even if it exaggerated the space allowed to traditionalists articulating the Church's current teaching. However, did any members of the Working Group really believe that the status quo is an option? If like me you come to the conclusion that the traditional condemnation of same-sex relationships is not right, then you are confronted with some challenges, including your understanding of Scripture.

Reverting to George Carey's remark in General Synod in July 1997, the tensions are indeed irreconcilable and in that not much has changed in twenty years. I fear both sides in the debate appear to have drawn a line in the sand. Both believe the other is wrong, but yet may agree to disagree. However, I detect some movement between the parties. More are now prepared to be accepting of gay relationships, even if they cannot fully affirm them. That said an increasing number *are* prepared to be affirming of them, with the canonical consequence that ultimately means for the Church.

It is this process of listening and exploring Scripture, tradition, reason and experience, which will be key in the months and years ahead. I am optimistic for the progress of the Shared Conversations and will play whatever part I can to help ensure they are as constructive as possible.

It would be an understatement to point out that the Church of England is noted for caution over change. One only has to consider the evidence presented by the progress towards legislating for women bishops, a process underpinned by some fine theological scholarship. The Synod agreed at an early point in the process that there was no theological objection to the ordination of women bishops and spent most of its time dealing with those who could not accept such a development. However, over this particular issue it is doubtful whether further scholarship will aid the debate. In some ways the debate has already gone beyond one of biblical interpretation and become a matter of ecclesiology and church order. I long for the energy that continues to be spent on those same Bible verses to be directed instead towards a workable theology for same-sex relationships. Indeed, I long for a Church where all, with integrity, can embrace our LGBTI brothers and sisters in Christ, rather than one where the unspoken issues continue to cloud the picture and a lack of honesty permeates relationships between those holding the starkly different viewpoints.

Chapter 5

Evangelicals, Gender and the New Jerusalem

Jody Stowell, Vicar of St Michaels and All Angels', Harrow Weald

Where do I Begin?

I became a Christian (in the traditional Evangelical 'Pray the Prayer' sense) when I was 14. I had grown up in a family of mixed spirituality, where we attended church until I was about 5, when we then seemed to just fall out of the habit. From then on my own spirituality took its understanding from the snippets of church that you inevitably received as someone growing up in the UK in the 80s.

I found myself in an Evangelical Anglican church by accident, with no idea that I had made a fundamental choice about my Christian identity. As I grew in my faith and in my knowledge of church politics and tribes, I began to better understand and appreciate what it meant to be an Evangelical, as well as an Anglican.

I have to admit I never felt comfortable with the traditional position on homosexuality. That said, I took seriously the need to live under the authority of both Church and Scripture. It is likely also true that I found that the subject was not one that impacted me directly, and so would have been happily able to live with this discomfort – believing it to be part of the discipline to which I had committed myself.

However, as I began to become further involved in wider church politics, in particular the conversation about gender, I became suddenly aware that there was, surprisingly to me, another option. This was aided by more in-depth study whilst embarking on my first degree in theology. Indeed, I believe that the link between gender and sexuality cannot be extricated from one another, although they are not of course synonymous. In fact, I found that I could not do the biblical work that I was doing on gender and avoid the question of sexuality.

Ordained Evangelical Woman

Personally, I don't feel that I can talk about my journey on the subject of sexuality without talking about what it means to talk about it as a woman, and in particular as an ordained Evangelical woman.

It is a subject of surprise to people that it often seems to be only men who are talking about this subject. Indeed, people often ask me if I know more women who would write or talk on this subject. 'T'was ever thus' I hear you cry! However, it is not only the gender bias which makes this a particularly difficult subject to get women to speak about.

As Evangelical women, we are already in jeopardy – as ordained Evangelical women, we are in double jeopardy.

An Evangelical woman lives with the embedded cultural reality that has been spoken over her – that she is there to 'help the man' and that he is the ultimate judge in 'matters to be decided'. She is told over and again in both words and culture that the men are in charge. What is more, she is constantly reminded that is how it *should* be. Being both Evangelical and a woman is already a challenge to our personhood and identity as a female human.

An ordained Evangelical woman experiences that conflict. As an Evangelical, she is expected to accept her place, and then *increases* this dissonance between who she is and her belonging in her tribe by becoming an ordained person. It causes underlying anxiety if there is a continued desire to belong. As a result, many women leave the tribe.

Many evangelicals have described the ordaining of women as 'The thin end of the wedge'. The charge that ordained women are 'the wedge' through which gay sex will be accepted in the church, has kept many women silent. If ordained evangelical women begin to talk about changing their mind on sexuality, then they can feel that their very being would probably be put at risk. Most have a sense of having already risked enough by being ordained, especially when their tribal family is ambivalent about the reality of their existence.

When 'Evangelical' is part of our identity, the risk feels rather high.

And yet the truth is that ordained Evangelical women know

first-hand that we cannot close the door on revisiting Scripture in the direction of fuller inclusion. We might say that we are not yet convinced, but we can never with integrity say that the matter is concluded.

My own journey with regards to sexuality and the place of LGBTI people in our Church is informed by the sheer hypocrisy that I feel I would have to own if I were ever to say that I was included and they were not. That I made it through the door by the skin of my teeth and then slammed it behind me!

This of course in itself does not make a new theology of sexuality, but it has and does give me pause whenever I am tempted to think I am an objective 'Keeper of the Keys'.

Gender and a New Jerusalem

The primary biblical text that I look to with regard to gender and sexuality is found in Genesis 1–3. This is because, for me, it is the lens through which I look at the rest of the biblical narrative.

In Genesis we find the story of the non-gendered human being, the dustling (*ha'adam*), who is made from the dust, and for whom it is 'not good to be alone'. The dustling sleeps and in waking finds the other human, in the face of whom, he is defined as 'he'. The poem that spills out from the newly defined man in Genesis 2 is a beautiful literary device in which the male human recognises both the sameness

'Bone of my bones and flesh of my flesh'

and the distinctiveness

'This one shall be called Woman, for out of Man this one was taken'

of the other human.

From this text we can see the suggestion that both genders are full representatives of humanity – men and women are of the same kind, they are of the same bone and flesh. Significantly, however, there is also a need for us to understand that our own definition is found most profoundly in the face of an 'other'. That in order for us to know ourselves more fully, we have to engage in a meeting of persons with other human beings. To be alone is to become smaller versions of ourselves.

Of course the otherness which is focussed upon in the poem in Chapter 2 is the significant otherness of gender. It is an appropriate symbol, as gender is one of the most visible signs of 'otherness' that we recognise in the variety of human beings, together perhaps with ethnicity.

However, it is not a *necessary* interpretation of the text that we might find a deeper knowledge of ourselves *only* in the face of someone of the opposite sex. Just as in fact it is not a necessary interpretation of the text that all must marry in order to have that meeting of persons through which we know our-self better.

If we stay in Genesis a bit longer, we may also reflect on the cultural attachment that we have as Western Christians in particular, to the Garden of Eden. I have often heard it suggested that we are 'returning' to the Garden of Eden, where all was perfect, before the disobedience of Adam and Eve ruined it all.

Although there is now a better understanding of the eschatological end towards which we are all moving, with the recognition that we are headed towards a New Jerusalem rather than backwards to the Garden of Eden, I don't think that the deep attachment that we have to the Garden of Eden can be underestimated.

In Western Christianity there has been an articulation of the Christian story from the Garden, through the Fall, to Redemption and ultimately Salvation, which indicates that the state of salvation is akin to the pre-fall Garden bliss. In other words, all was perfect until we messed it up, Jesus came and now it is moving towards perfect again. And so although we know in our heads that we are headed for the City, our hearts are often dreaming of the Garden.

In contrast the narrative of Eastern Christianity begins with the Garden being 'good', as the biblical text states, with the intention that there was always a journey towards being perfected in Christ. Instead of perfection returning to perfection, the story moves from goodness, through disobedience, redemption, salvation, perfection. The Garden was always headed towards the City. Humanity was always headed towards a New Humanity.

In focusing on the onward journey towards the eschatological reality, I find that there is a certain unknowing about what that means for the nature of humanity. This can feel disturbing. It can feel especially disturbing if we have a picture of perfection in which binary categories of male and female are the ultimate forms of humanity.

Whether or not we believe that we will retain gender, I want to suggest that is not a necessary interpretation of Scripture. In the unknowing journey towards the New Jerusalem there is a possibility that the conversation that is now being conducted on gender and sexuality, particularly with regards to the fluidity of gender and the new knowledge that we have about intergender conditions, is going to show us something of the *new* humanity towards which we are headed.

In terms of my own journey in thinking about sexuality and gender, this focus on the eschatological, means that whilst the first human order teaches us something and is significant, I am not absolutely convinced that it is the ultimate form or 'end' of humanity.

Are there things that we can know then? The unknowing is contingent on the knowing that God is good and the imperative upon us to encounter other human beings as those made in the image of God. The ethic of our sexuality is constrained by those truths proclaimed throughout Scripture. Of course there are other truths, however what I am suggesting is that there is freedom, and indeed an imperative, to explore what the biblical story tells us about gender and sexuality, beyond the usual rhetoric.

Personal Reflection on the Stories of Jesus

As an Evangelical I proclaim that Scripture, read in the power of the Holy Spirit, is a living word to us, through which we can gain understanding of what it means to be people of this particular God: who should I be and what should I do? I have therefore aimed to give an indication of the way in which I approach Scripture and the seriousness with which I take it all.

But the ultimate Living Word to us is Jesus, whom I know by the Spirit. It is in the stories in Scripture where I find Jesus encountering all manner of human beings, that I find my journey on the issue of sexuality really comes to bear.

At heart I fear I am a bit of a coward. I want to belong to my Evangelical tribe and although I am Open Evangelical and therefore love to affirm and include in my own spirituality the disciplines and practices that I find in other traditions which nourish me, I am an Evangelical. There is a part of me that would like to just keep my head down and be accepted as 'one of the boys'.

This is where Scripture deals with my heart problem.

In the stories where Jesus tells the religious that they have not understood Scripture, that they are using it to perpetuate their own system, their own status quo, their own worldview (e.g. Mark 7), this is where I am undone. I must challenge my desire to belong as the lens through which I interpret Scripture.

The other place in Scripture which speaks to me is the story in which Jesus heals a man on the Sabbath (Mark 3). Again those who have interpreted Scripture in a particular way are challenged by Jesus for staying silent when asked whether he should heal on the Sabbath. In fact, and this is what I find the most alarming, Jesus is 'grieved at their hardness of heart'. Reading this Scripture was one of the most liberating and disturbing moments in my own journey on sexuality. Rather than speaking about a 'position' on healing on the Sabbath, the passage speaks about those who refuse to look again at Scripture and in so doing who grieve Jesus by their hardness of heart. I found it disturbing because it spoke to my own desire to stay silent and wait for someone else to speak, and I found it liberating because I finally knew that I would rather risk being wrong with a soft heart, than to grieve Jesus with my hard heart.

Conclusion

I cannot let my desire to belong be more important than being willing to take the risk of seeking after the way of grace and truth. There have been times in my journey where I have been tempted to think my own private thoughts and do my own journey in my head, where it is safer...for me. These stories challenge my desire for my own comfort, against the need to do the hard work of thinking through this issue and then to have an open conversation about it.

As Evangelicals I believe we desperately need to be allowed to have the conversation. Even if we do that at risk of being 'expelled', then we must still do it anyway.

Chapter 6

Ever, Honestly, Truly Me

Hayley Matthews, Rector of Holy Innocents', Fallowfield

Anxiously, I watched as the woman dressed in various shades of pink and beige closed the door, checking it was tightly shut. She 'sealed it' in prayer, and began to do the same with the windows. She needed to ensure, she said, that nothing evil would escape the room, and that nothing evil could come in. The woman beside me patted me with a warm hand. Mine were freezing. I'd been ill for months after contracting salmonella and was still struggling to eat properly, but even so, I'd been told to undertake a complete fast for three full days, drinking only water, to ensure the best possible outcome from this 'deliverance'. Yes, I was cold; and wobbly, and frightened. I was twenty-six years old.

Two years previously, nothing could have prepared me for the way in which Jesus entered my vaguely Christian and seekingly spiritual life. Not so much with a gentle unfolding, but in all His glory and joy, 'I was SAVED, hallelujah!' Neither did anything prepare me for the fact that for months I would not be able to watch the news, or hear people lying and cheating, or see the homeless and the 'care in the community' and the addict without my heart breaking. There was no denying Jesus was real, divine, entering into the hearts and lives of His people here in the 21st century.

As a young woman of cynicism, pragmatism and logic my new found faith knocked me off my feet. None of it 'made sense' and I set about reading the Bible and buying concordances for all I was worth, given that suddenly I had been caught up into something so undeniable, unshakeable and life-altering that I had to understand it.

The bedrest and recuperation resulting from the salmonella were actually a blessing in disguise It gave me time to immerse myself in the Scriptures – translating every last word with my concordances beside me. I prayed; I worshipped; I even taught myself to play the guitar because I could not get to church. I asked people to bring me recorded teachings and sermons, and sat listening to entire services. I was virtually 'lowered down on a mat' whenever I was well enough by friends. I was nothing if not dedicated to knowing the God who had so radically changed my life – both my inner life and my entire world view.

After two full years of intense focus I felt that I knew the Lord's love (the Lord's compassion towards His creation and individuals), the Lord's Spirit at work in the world (by no means at least within me), and the Scriptures inside out and back to front in a way in which I wish I had capacity to, today, as a priest. I didn't need a cross referenced bible because in those days, I was able to do that, by God's grace, in a heartbeat. I say this, not to show-off, but to let you know that I haven't wandered into this discussion half-baked with a superficial understanding of it all. I have been as robust as I possibly can be, scripturally, spiritually and psychologically. I have endeavoured to be open to the fact that I might be completely and utterly mistaken in my views, and that I might in fact need 'to change'.

And I *was* willing to change into whatever my Lord would have me be – that is, until it appeared that this might actually be the priesthood, which, for somebody who dared not read a lesson, seemed somewhat on the impossible side, to my mind. My heart was broken over and over as it was changed from a 'heart of stone' – and continues to be changed – to a 'heart of flesh'. I began to care about everyone and everything. I learned to cry; to suffer; to persevere; to rejoice again; to live with joy whatever the circumstances, and to be willing to be plunged into that cycle over and over again in many and various contexts for both my own and other's sakes.

My first calling was to that of intercession. My partner and I had been summarily thrown out of church on discovery of our deeper relationship despite the continual acceptance by most within the church that 'God has brought you two together in such an amazing way in your ministry'. I always found it odd that people would speak of God's evident grace being seen in and through our ministry whilst we were in a loving, monogamous and committed same-sex relationship, albeit a hidden one, but then how quickly this was condemned when a fact people had been at pains to deny became unavoidable. And so, bereft of my church family who had become my life over two years of regular ministry, I prayed. To be more accurate – I wept and I prayed: 'My God, my God, why have you forsaken me?' And in response He just kept weeping with me, whispering, 'Love them; love them; love my people,'. I knew that this meant accepting where they were whilst persevering in showing them where I believed the Spirit was at work in an Acts 10 manner. At the same time, I was also being called into loving 'my' people, too: 'Tell them about Me – tell them, that I love them and I do not reject them. Remember, I was an outcast, too!'

After a few months I summoned my courage and decided to go back to another church to try again. Despite the profound sense of assurance I felt from God in relation to my sexuality, the church did not concur. So I went to see if they couldn't help me to be the person *they* said Jesus wanted me to be. I was more than willing to submit 'to the authority of Scripture', 'to the authority of the Church', 'to the authority of the Vicar/pastor/preacher/learned other'. 'Lean not unto your own understanding...' Loving God with all of my heart and soul and understanding, there was nothing I would not submit to my Lord and my God.

So, there I was, waiting for this dreadful demon of homosexuality to be cast out of me. Would it be the big black snake they had suggested it might be? Would I be sick in a bucket? Would I writhe on the floor or spit and swear at them like those things in the books they had loaned me? I was more afraid of such things than they could possibly have known. How would I get through it? Would it hurt? What if they weren't strong enough and there was a battle? What if they couldn't get it out? *Help me Jesus! Help me, please!*

So the prayer began. Nothing happened. We prayed some more, or more precisely they did as I passively awaited my deliverance. Still nothing. I began to feel joy rising within me, and I accidentally giggled. The room sealer took this as a bad sign and the prayer became more fervent. Suddenly, I could hold it in no longer, but songs of the Spirit flowed from my lips and the woman with the warm hand began to laugh, too. 'There's nothing wrong with her!' she exclaimed, 'She's singing to the Lord' and how she roared with laughter, filing the room with it.

The other woman looked somewhat piqued and a little embarrassed. She made an attempt at explaining that probably the fast had been enough on its own, to 'heal' me, warning me to be very, very careful over the coming days and weeks as 'it' could quickly enter back into me, finding the house swept clean. But at that moment, I knew it was untrue. I knew that God was and is and had been with me all along and that the sleepless nights lying awake worrying about having something evil inside of me was a lie, and that it was the lie that was evil and controlling and dangerous, hedging me about with unGodly fear. At that moment, Jesus set me free indeed, although it took some years for me to live in the fullness of that freedom, and more especially, to feel able to openly express it.

Delivered from fear by Perfect Love, my life changed inextricably. Continuing to rip the Scriptures limb from limb in my efforts to truly grasp to Whom I was bound, an inner assurance grew and grew – I was loved, *without* caveats. My worth was equitable with my brothers and sisters; I was not 'less than', damaged or disabled, or worse still, tainted by an inherent sin always lurking in the background. I was a whole human being, created in the image of God, fully alive in Christ, living, breathing, worshipping, and serving Jesus as our Lord and Saviour. I became Hayley, daughter, woman, neighbour and friend, not *sotto voce* 'Hayley, y'know…' or as I had more than once encountered variations of, 'oh! Hello! Are you Hayley-the-lesbian?' often with some sense of incredulity that I did not fit stereotypes and appeared to be, well, genuinely charismatic. What on earth was the Holy Spirit thinking?

Meanwhile, I was removed from all rotas apart from the 'delivering leaflets' rota. Whatever the good Lord had done for me, in church I knew my place. I was conscious that, irrespective of the 'love the sinner hate the sin' rhetoric, no other 'sinners' were sanctioned by exclusion or a meritocracy of role/service. Celibate or not, I was 'less than'. From there, the parish and I went on a long journey together, and learned to love one another and be fully inclusive to the point that I was leading a worship team for Sunday morning worship, amongst other things.

For almost a decade I remained faithful to my calling above all else, and eventually found myself – to my utter disbelief – training to enter the priesthood at Ridley Hall in Cambridge. In retrospect my lay ministry utterly consumed my life – fulfilling, meaningful and Christ-centred as it was – so the lack of loving intimacy was kept at bay and possibly even hidden by the joy of serving God and God's people. But all that was to change when I moved away from all of my support networks, my busy parish life and into what was a surprisingly hostile environment for women, at the time. Suddenly, my 'me' was 'in my face' and I was once again confronted with the juxtaposition of an intense calling and divine inner assurance that I was loved as I am (without the celibacy caveat) standing in direct contrast to the overt hostility and often shocking homophobia openly expressed in lectures, in prayer and in conversation. Having been in a parish church that became increasingly open and warm and accepting of me (and others) as a person, if not the breadth of sexual orientation itself, it was devastating to see it operating that intensely at that level. These people would be Church leaders and could hurt many – particularly the young and vulnerable.

Theological studies gave way to psychological and biological studies eventually leading me to my recent PhD, *No Faith in Equality and Diversity*, from a management perspective. I had no choice but to move beyond the Scriptures if I was to understand what God was assuring me of in direct contrast to the constant chipping away (nay, hammering) endured year on year from many and varied parts of the Church. However, I began to be gently and silently loved by more traditional churches and eventually found a home in the liberal catholic (or now, I might be so bold as to describe my church as very gently charismatic catholic) wing of our faith.

This was an enormous grief and a huge challenge for me, entering into an entirely new world with its own cultural challenges and my own lack of expertise, in order to be free to exercise my ministry as myself, and possibly more importantly, as an inclusive priest towards those outside of or having left the Church on the grounds of their sexuality or gender. I had to find God again in a strange and barren (as it at first appeared to me) land.

The journey has been heartbreaking for all sorts of reasons., I remain now single – accepting that my time has probably been and gone whilst I was busy rejecting some beautiful, Godly, loving suitors for fidelity's sake. However, the journey across the traditions of the Church has been life-giving and I hope has made me a far better priest than ever I would have been had I remained in my 'comfort zone', operating from my strengths. I could not see its weaknesses until I had spent enough time 'over here' to look across and see things from another angle. I could not see the good in ritualised liturgy until I grew to know and love the liturgical year and how Jesus' life and gift to us in Himself are so beautifully framed and celebrated in such poignant and joyful ways. It is interesting to reflect that this is yet another form of exclusion where so often we can, as Evangelicals, choose to lambast and exclude, judge and ridicule our own brothers and sisters in Christ.

Aside from academic papers, spiritual seeking and theological and doctrinal rigour, if I am honest there has been one key factor in continuing to know God's favour – at every point where I have suppressed, denied, hidden, been ashamed of or rejected a non-heteronormative sexual orientation, God's presence has simply disappeared from my life. No matter how faithful, active and honest I am in all other realms, the denial of personal relationship and the *possibility* of love (whether or not it is either found or acted upon) has culminated in a denial of God. This inextricable link also works the other way round. When I embrace the LGBTI community in work or ministry, in friendship and/or relationship, when I allow myself to love (should there ever be occasion to) – God's grace and Spirit is almost overwhelming. Few and far between as moments of genuine love for me, from one adult to another, have been, I have known in those moments God's love for me in a way I have never experienced at any other time.

Sadly, much more often, I have felt the Lord's sadness, over another suicide, another broken relationship, another person afraid to be themselves, or one who feels they must 'decide' between Church and their own mental health, for no-one can continually deny or fracture themselves without risking a serious impact on their health and wellbeing.

The world has changed. I refer not to her morals or legislatively (although that is undeniably true), but in her learning. In her seeking after the understanding of what it is to be human and what makes us tick. We have entered into a journey of discovery about our genetic and psychological development over many thousands of years, and now are far more aware about how we have come to understand ourselves as spiritual and physical and often sexual beings.

It is hard, having one's certitudes shaken, but they are certitudes. Jesus Christ is the *only* true and living Word. What 'Word' simply repeats itself over and over ad infinitum without ever listening to the voice of the beloved or entering into the deepest of dialogues where we seek to know one another, to learn and grow in one another's sunshine and shadow? Not the Jesus I know, that's for sure.

44

Outside

I see you from a distance –
It's a chasm I can't cross
As you look upon my filthiness,

                    my life,
                              my friends,
                                        my dross,

Then you tell me that He loves me
As you tidy me away,
Tucking in my collar and throwing things away…
The panic rises in my throat
                    As my real self spins away
While I'm patted on the head and told,
'You're much nicer this way.'

Yet now the chasm's wider
As fear builds in my head…
I wanted life, love, freedom,
So how come I've wound up dead?

I thought that Jesus knew me,
I thought He'd understand,
I thought He'd love me as I am and hold my dirty hand
And now I dare not turn to Him
To show what I've become…

Oh give me back my life,
                    my friends,
                              my filthiness and dross
For then I can come honestly
Beneath Your mighty cross!
And as I kneel there, broken, in the clothes I shouldn't wear,
From a place that stays unspoken,
With a love I mustn't share,
I feel You cross the chasm
And lift me to my feet,
You brush the dirt from off my face
And for the very first time I meet…

The Eyes that do accept me,
That tell me of my worth,

That ask me if I'm ready for each step of this new birth.
The Feet that wait there patiently
When I stop and hesitate,
The Feet that will run after me
If I bolt and turn away.
The Mouth that smiles right through my dross
And makes me feel brand new
Speaking words of love and wisdom,
Oh my Jesus, words so true.

And even as my collar is tucked,
While I'm chastened and told and tutted and clucked,
You whisper strength and love and hope
Until a song is rising in my throat
That soars in worship to the One
Who didn't strip me dangerously bare
Or give me a coverall to wear.

Oh give me grace to do the same,
To love the unlovely in their shame,
Patiently walking at their pace
Not afraid to touch their dirty face.
And Lord, I pray you, let me be,
Ever, honestly, truly me.

Chapter 7

A Credible Witness

Gavin Collins, Archdeacon of the Meon

What We are 'Supposed to Think!'

'Heaven help us when even the Vicars don't know what they are supposed to think!' – these words have haunted me since they were muttered in my direction at the end of a New Wine seminar led by the Evangelical Alliance's Theological Consultant in the run-up to the passing of the Marriage (Same Sex Couples) Act 2013. After a long presentation on why the establishment of same-sex marriage was felt to be catastrophic from a Christian and moral point of view, the floor (or, rather, the tent) was opened to questions. I asked the final question, and simply admitted that, as a Church leader, I was struggling with the whole issue of *why* same-sex relationships were not permitted. I explained that given that we had already agreed to depart from 2 out of the 3 key elements of the traditional Christian understanding of marriage (one man with one woman, for life, for the procreation of children), then I was striving to understand what was so distinctive about the 'one man with one woman' element that rendered that absolute for all time and in all circumstances, when we were prepared to recognise and conduct marriages that breached the 'for life' and 'for the procreation of children' elements. The speaker was unable to give me an answer, and the seminar ended, whereupon I was surprised to find myself at the centre of a group of about 15 people, holding an impromptu discussion, with one person thanking me for having 'had the courage' to ask the question they had wanted to ask, but did not feel the environment was free or open enough for them to do so. As we talked, one person walked past and deliberately muttered their chilling sotto voce verdict: *'Heaven help us when even the Vicars don't know what they are supposed to think!'* Those words struck me deeply, and have remained with me ever since, as there is patently an unwillingness and an inability amongst Evangelicals to engage openly, rigorously and Biblically with this vital missional and pastoral issue.

Wrestling with the Bible's Application to those who Experience Same-Sex Attraction

For a number of years I held to a 'traditional' understanding that the physical expression of a same-sex relationship was simply not Biblically permissible, and that the only valid options for a sexual relationship were heterosexual marriage or celibacy. I satisfied myself that this was not discriminatory against those with same-sex attraction, as heterosexuals were also not permitted sexual activity outside of marriage. However, this, of course, ignored the reality that a heterosexual person had a potential Biblically mandated context for a sexual relationship, and ceased altogether to be a valid argument once the legal possibility of same-sex marriage arrived in 2013. If the traditional view were to remain valid, then I realised that I had to be able to understand and articulate a clear argument as to why the Bible mandated that the only permissible form of sexual activity was within a heterosexual marriage.

Romans Chapter 1 is perhaps the clearest Biblical prohibition against homosexual sex, but, even without going into the tortuous disputes as to the precise meanings of the Greek words used there, that does not explain *why* such activity is prohibited as being symptomatic of rebellion against God, merely states the fact *that* it is. In the run up to the passing of the Civil Partnerships Act in 2004, and for several years thereafter, I wrestled long and hard in an attempt to articulate a clear Biblical understanding of *why* same-sex sexual relationships were beyond the pale in Scriptural terms.

Far too often, there is a conspiracy of silence, fearfulness and victimisation on this subject. How on earth have we reached the point where we have allowed someone's views on same-sex relationships to become the defining criterion on their 'soundness' as an Evangelical, or even their most basic status as a fellow Christian? And the way in which whenever an Evangelical has had the courage to ask questions or seek to open a Biblical debate on this topic, they have been instantly written off and cast out, serves to close down honest debate, splinter fellowship and denigrate fellow members of the body of Christ.

The Credibility of Our Witness

Another formative experience for me came 4 or 5 years ago, when

I was with a youth group at Soul Survivor. I was talking late one evening with a dozen or so of the teenagers – all of whom had come from a traditional, rigorously Evangelical Church, with a good understanding of Scripture and of Christian doctrine. The subject of same-sex relationships came up, and I was staggered at the extent to which, for this group of 14–18 year olds, it simply was *not* an issue. Indeed, they just could not understand or connect with why the Church felt the need to be adamantly opposed to all expressions of same-sex relationships. I became acutely aware of not only how little traditional Christian teaching on this area connected with the emerging generation, but also how the gulf this led to in our perceived relevance to contemporary society presented a huge and urgent challenge for us in terms of our witness and credibility to the world around us.

I was not at this stage seeking to depart from a traditional understanding of sexuality and ethics, but rather was beginning to appreciate the need to be able to articulate that teaching in a way that was credible and defensible before a rightly questioning and increasingly sceptical world.

'Not Good to be Alone'

One of the foundational passages for the traditional understanding of heterosexual marriage is the account in Genesis 2. Having repeatedly assured us that all that He has made is good, God then says it is *not* good for man to be alone and so creates Eve as a companion for Adam. It is worth noting that God recognises the importance of this need, even in perfect Eden, and given no suitable companion for him to be found from amongst the other animals provides a unique 'helpmeet' – rather than a group of friends. For some years, I had reached the conclusion that this pointed to the need for heterosexual marriage, so that man and woman could each find fulfilment on the human level in someone who was 'same, but different' to him or herself: The need to be of the same species in order to have sufficient affinity of relationship, but the differentiation of sex showing that fulfilment was found in someone 'different' from oneself. I saw this as key as otherwise it became a form of 'self-fulfilment', which would be getting close to the essence of idolatry – especially perhaps when the sacramental function of marriage as per Ephesians 5 is considered.

However, the testimony of numerous homosexual friends has persuasively convinced me that there is no element of idolatry or finding 'fulfilment in self' involved in their relationships. Instead there is a sense – and often, at first at least, a deeply unwelcomed, certainly unsought for sense – of finding the deepest human partnership, connection and fulfilment in someone of the same sex. Whatever the originating cause may be – and I am not at all qualified to comment on debates about nature or nurture or any other potential determining factors in same-sex attraction – the plain and evident reality is that for a significant number of people today the deepest 'connection' on a human level – emotionally, psychologically, relationally and physically – is found in someone of the same sex, rather than someone of the opposite sex. This is a reality that the Church needs to acknowledge, and work out a coherent, defensible and pastoral response to. And, as an Evangelical, it is my firm commitment and conviction that that response must be shaped by Scripture, and that we are not free either to bend or to ignore elements of Scripture just because we find them unpalatable or uncomfortable in the context of our contemporary world.

1 Corinthians 7 and Matthew 19 Applied to those with Same-Sex Attraction

In wrestling with the above tension, I found myself increasingly returning to 1 Corinthians 7, and Paul's teaching about marriage and singleness. Writing to a heterosexual context, Paul clearly teaches that it is better for a person to remain single/celibate, so that they can be more free to concentrate on the things of the Kingdom (vv.8, 32–35 and 37–38). However, Paul acknowledges the reality of sexual drive, temptation and lust, and therefore as a concession to human nature concedes that it is permissible – even desirable – for someone who does not have the gift or the strength of self-control to remain chastely single, to go ahead and marry. This was deemed preferable to what would for the majority of people be the inevitable alternative, i.e. immorality and sexual activity outside of marriage.

The defining moment for me in this whole debate came when I began to ask the question of how 1 Corinthians 7 should apply to those who experience same-sex attractedness? The traditional Church position has been to say that the only Biblically valid option is celibacy – as exemplified commendably by commitment of the 'Living Out' organisation. However, St Paul himself says, in the context of writing to heterosexual believers, that the reality of the human sex drive is such that celibacy is not a realistic or sustainable option for many, perhaps the majority, of people, and that it is therefore better for them to go ahead and be married. As such they can then live in a context of a faithful, committed relationship, rather than the most likely alternative of unfaithfulness and transitory sexual relationships without meaningful commitment.

In his reflection with the disciples following his verbal joust with the Pharisees on divorce and remarriage in Matthew 19:1–12, Jesus makes exactly the same point, and says that, while celibacy and singleness may be the better option from a Kingdom perspective, 'not everyone can accept this...but only those to whom it has been given...The one who can accept this should accept it.' (vv.11–12).

I fail to see how it can possibly be a Biblically valid standpoint for the Church to require a standard of behaviour from same-sex attracted Christians that in both of these key passages the Bible itself says many/most of us who are heterosexual are inevitably not able to live up to ourselves. – Jesus' teaching on logs and specks in the eye comes forcibly to mind here. Indeed, I would go further and say that for the Church to impose a forced celibacy or require heterosexual marriage as the only valid options for someone with a deep rooted same-sex attractedness who does not have the gift/strength of celibacy, is both practically and pastorally unrealistic. In my opinion it is doomed to promote either sin, in the form of immorality and promiscuity, or else dissonance, psychological dishonesty and potentially serious psychological harm. That simply cannot be a tenable position for the Church to be in from any possible standpoint, be that Biblical, pastoral, safeguarding or simple human respect and compassion.

Therefore, in seeking to apply the reality and pragmatic acceptance of human nature that underlies 1 Corinthians 7 and Matthew 19 to those with a same-sex attractedness, I find myself compelled to conclude that for those who have the gift or strength of self-control to remain celibate, then that is presumably the 'better way', just as it is also for those with a heterosexual attractedness. For many/most, however, that will not be the case and therefore – following Paul's argument in vv.9, 36 & 38 of 1 Corinthians 7 – in order to save them from sin, severe psychological dissonance, and the inevitable recurring experience of 'falling short' and 'failing', it is right/better/necessary for them to be able to live out their same-sex attractedness in a context that is rooted in and able to express the God-given qualities of loving, faithful commitment.

Same-Sex Partnership or Marriage?

For some while during the public debate in the lead up to the Marriage (Same Sex Couples) Act 2013, I was content to support the idea of formal recognition of same sex couples, but felt it wrong to confuse that with the description 'marriage'. However, I have become increasingly aware of how unclear Scripture is as to what constitutes a valid marriage (e.g. the polygamous nature of many of the marriages of the Old Testament patriarchs). Add to that the fact that the majority of the Church has recognised that it can be right in appropriate circumstances to recognise/permit/conduct marriages following divorce and/or where there is no intention/ability for procreation and childbirth, and I now find myself asking myself what was so uniquely distinctive about the 'one man, one woman' element of the traditional Christian definition of marriage as being between: 'one man and one woman, for life, for the procreation of children'?

For me – as someone who is committed to taking an overall Biblical theology view of the sweep of Scripture on this subject – my conclusion is that the hallmarks of marriage must be a public declaration/intention to live in a relationship of commitment, love and faithfulness. I acknowledge the realities of sin, pride and fall-enness, and hence the reality of divorce, and the legitimacy of a second marriage in appropriate circumstances – whilst seeking always to avoid the danger of blessing adultery or condoning 'serial polygamy'. As a pastoral minister, I am delighted to officiate at the marriage of couples who, through age or disability, know that they will not be able to have children. This is also the case for those for whom the decision not to seek to have children has come as a result of considered discussion and deliberation. For me, it has therefore become a logical and right step to move away also from the third traditional plank of 'one man and one woman', and to concentrate instead on the inherent qualities that mark out Christian marriage, i.e. love, faithfulness and commitment.

A further turning point for me was hearing a very moving description during the passing of the 2013 Act, of a lesbian broadcaster describing her relationship with her partner, and realising that her deeply felt need to be able to describe her monogamous, committed relationship as a 'marriage' was far greater than any felt need that I had to deny her that title.

Standing on the Side of Public Commitment

In the context of the current Church of England debate, I have come to the conclusion that for the well-being of the individuals concerned, the sake of moral integrity and honesty on the part of the Church, the acknowledgment of relational reality, and – perhaps above all else – for the sake of the credibility of our compassionate witness to our nation – it is important that we not only 'permit' the validity of same-sex relationships, but that we move to the point where we are able to affirm, celebrate and stand alongside couples as they enter into them.

Our God is a God of loving, faithful commitment, and where a couple – straight or gay – seek to live in a relationship that reflects and expresses those qualities of love, faithfulness and commitment, then it must be right for the Church not only to permit that, but indeed positively to affirm, celebrate and bless it: Commitment has always been hard, but perhaps never more so than in today's transitory society. Part of our calling as a Church is to stand with those throughout our society who are seeking publicly to live lives of loving commitment, which as St Paul acknowledges in his advice to the Corinthians may be found in more than one validly permissible alternative. However, what simply is not tenable is to set a standard for others that both the Bible and my direct experience consistently teaches me is one that I would be unable to live within for myself.

First Order or Second Order?

I would make a brief comment about the extent to which this can validly be seen as a first order issue. The view one takes on the permissibility of same-sex relationships has increasingly become a defining test of orthodoxy amongst Evangelicals, and in some quarters even a test of whether one can validly be considered to be a Christian at all. Whilst there are clear disagreements between theologians and Biblical scholars as to the meaning and right application of the various key Bible passages, I simply fail to see how that can legitimately be taken as grounds for writing someone off as having strayed beyond the fold. I was brought up in an Evangelical context in which we were taught to have a robust view of Scripture, and to treat the Bible with enough respect to approach it rigorously and wrestle scripturally over difficult issues, rather than being satisfied – or acting as if Scripture was satisfied – with rote-learnt pat or 'proper' answers that failed to engage with the grittiness, difficulties and confusion of the world and this life.

On all sides of this discussion, there are far too many fellow Christians who I respect too much to write them all off just because we may have reached different conclusions on this topic. It is frequently said that the younger one is in faith, the greater the felt need for simple, black and white answers. The experience of life and of walking in faith with God is that the reality of the world is far less clear and far more grey, and that God is to be found in the midst of that confusion and mess. Indeed, I believe He calls us to be prepared to walk with Him in that gracious and humble uncertainty. We also have to acknowledge the existence in the Church at times of very real, and latent homophobia and prejudice – especially, I would assess, in older generations – that serves to colour and distort much of our thinking, or unpreparedness to think, on this issue.

Return to Ephesians 5 and the Sacramental Potential of Marriage

I want to end by returning to Ephesians 5, and Paul's teaching on the sacramental potential of marriage (and I am sufficiently Evangelical to insist that it is Paul who is teaching the Ephesians!). Paul was writing in a context where the only possible covenantal expression of commitment was heterosexual marriage. As such he calls any married Christian man and woman to appreciate the potential and the responsibility they have to live in such a way that their marriage relationship might point those around them to catch a glimpse of something of the covenantal, loving, faithful commitment of Christ to his Church. Holding this together with the reality that Paul affirms in 1 Corinthians 7 that for many/most people, the only viable options are marriage or promiscuity, and seeing just how desperately our broken world today needs to see lived out examples of the potential of faithful commitment, then my conviction is that as a Church we need to stand alongside and support *all* couples who desire to live in loving faithful commitment. This is true whether they be heterosexual or homosexual. In doing so I believe we enable all to see more of those core characteristics of God – love, faithfulness and commitment – manifested in our world today. As we do so, we will in turn enable the world to see more of God's presence and to know more of God's love in our midst.

Chapter 8

Desire, Intimacy and Discipleship

David Newman, Archdeacon of Loughborough

When I was a young single Christian, I remember being concerned about how I would know who was the right person to marry. My desire to get it right was dressed up in spiritual clothing. My faith determined that even such an affair of the heart had to be compatible with my first call to be a disciple of Jesus Christ. That said I am sure there were some underlying commitment anxieties too. In the end a wise friend suggested that I might know the answer when I was no longer asking the question which happily experience proved to be true. This will give you a brief glimpse into some of the traits of my personality. I tend to lead with the head rather than the heart. I am loyal to the status quo until convinced of change. I will commit with passion to people and causes but not 'carelessly, lightly or selfishly but reverently, responsibly and after serious thought', to use the solemn words of the marriage service. My journey of understanding and accepting homosexual relationships has been similarly cautious. I share that journey with the hesitation of one who knows what powerful reactions these issues can engender, yet convinced we need to pursue every way of open, scriptural dialogue.

The Challenge of a Highly Sexualised Culture

It was relatively easy to start out with a traditional evangelical understanding of homosexuality. If the over-sexualisation of life and relationships had begun, it wasn't yet in our faces in the way it is today. Sex was a much more private issue and gay people more hidden. Heterosexual norms could be assumed relatively unchallenged in a biblical view of sexuality which was summed up as chastity outside of marriage and faithfulness within it. This was essentially fair because it applied to everyone, heterosexual and homosexual alike. Outside of marriage everyone had to submit to the discipline of continence. Moreover, there were biblical texts to support the view that homosexual practice was wrong, and I could convince myself that there would always be enough divine grace to enable someone to obey God's will if they were serious about doing so.

Since then the world has changed. The sexualisation of relationships is as brash as ever and sexual desire is exploited shamelessly
for its commercial potential in a consumer society. The internet and
mobile phone have opened up new dimensions of sexual experience and behaviour. Internet pornography is widely viewed, and
sexting has been described as an epidemic in our schools with the
NSPCC suggesting that between 15 and 40 per cent of young people are involved depending on their age. One writer concludes 'The
media's marketing of sex, the cultural endorsement of the 'do what
feels good' mentality, the prevalence of pornography and the wide-
spread misunderstanding of sex that prompts people to chase after
love and acceptance in unhealthy physical relationships are all factors that make it difficult to practice chastity. The reality is chastity
is not the norm. And such a discipline is certainly not easy.'[19] We
may deeply regret this but it is the context with which our theology
and pastoral ethics have to engage.

Encounters with those of Different Sexual Identities

The other change for me has been my growing experience of engaging with gay people. I have come to know couples who are living
out their faith responsibly and fruitfully in a committed partnership.
If Jesus talked of judging people by their fruits then there would be
no reason to question their Christian integrity any more than that
of their heterosexual counterparts. Their relationships bear the fruit
of love, wisdom and spiritual commitment. Furthermore, I have
also become aware of the deep pain and suffering that has accompanied some who have struggled with issues of sexual identity. A
particularly memorable experience was attending a service at one
of the churches in my archdeaconry marking a transgender day of
remembrance for those who had lost their lives in acts of transpho-
bic violence. At the same time, we remembered transgender people
who had tragically taken their own lives.

It was a salutary reminder of several difficult realities. First there
are those for whom sexual identity is a much more complex issue
than a simple clear-cut male / female binary divide. Few will be

---

19   http://www.relevantmagazine.com/life/relationship/features/28337-the-
secret-sexual-revolution. This article quotes a US survey which claims that 88% of
unmarried young people (18–29) are having sex and that only goes down to 80%
for Christians

confronted with the sharpness of this as that felt by transgender people. Yet we are much more aware today of the spectrum of masculinity and femininity that lies within each one of us, and which we own and embrace with differing levels of acceptance and comfort. Secondly, however, the testimonies of those enduring suffering, persecution, and even killing indicate that many are threatened by issues of sexual identity. Deep fears can spill out in hostile, unloving and violent reactions. I was greatly moved by the gentleness and vulnerability of some the transgender people I met that night, and came away feeling how much I wanted the Church to be a loving and welcoming community to those who are seeking to integrate their sexuality into a mature discipleship.

Going Beyond a Simple 'No' to Intimacy: Jesus and Paul on Celibacy

In the light of the sexualised world out there, and the complex and often confusing inner world of people's sexual feelings and identity, I have increasingly felt that it is not sufficient for the Church to have just one answer for gay people in relation to same-sex intimacy – which is 'No'. If same-sex desire is just as real as heterosexual desire, and for most is a settled orientation rather than a temporary phase or disordered state from which they can be healed, then those who want to pursue a Christian lifestyle in which their sexual identity contributes to healthy self-regard and loving relationships need to hear more from the Church than denial or judgment. My old way of thinking – that chastity outside of marriage was fair because it applied to homosexuals and heterosexuals alike – began to seem less just, because there is always the possibility of marriage for heterosexuals, whereas homosexuals are simply pointed to the route of sexual abstinence. Moreover, the New Testament does not teach that chastity is a universal gift.

Both Jesus and Paul are very realistic about the possibility of celibacy. Jesus is clear that for some it may be part of the commitment to single-minded discipleship when he talks of those who have 'renounced marriage because of the kingdom of heaven.' His actual phrase is about being eunuchs which reinforces the point that this is abstinence from both marriage and sex. However, he concedes that this is not a universal calling as he adds the important qualification that 'Not everyone can accept this word, but only those to whom it has been given'.[20] Exactly what they are being given is not spelt out – whether it is the particular gifts and vision for ministry that transcends the need for marriage or the power of self-control that makes celibacy of this sort possible. It could well be both.

However, Paul is unambiguous when he ventures onto this territory as he writes to the church in Corinth. Those who choose the way of celibacy will need the gift of continence. He is enthusiastic about the advantages of singleness for the committed believer. 'I wish that all of you were as I am'. However, like Jesus he is aware that this is not for everybody. 'But each of you has your own gift from God; one has this gift, another has that.'[21] In fact he is extremely pragmatic about the need for channelling sexual desire into marriage. 'Since sexual immorality is occurring each man should have sexual relations with his own wife and each woman with her own husband', 'come together... so that Satan will not tempt you because of your lack of self-control' and perhaps most memorably 'But if they cannot control themselves, they should marry, for it is better to marry than to burn with passion'.[22]

It is not the most romantic picture of marriage. There is no talk of 'making love' here. In the Book of Common Prayer it finds expression in the second purpose of marriage as ordained 'for a remedy against sin and to avoid fornication; that such persons as have not the gift of continency might marry and keep themselves undefiled members of Christ' body.' We have rightly given the idea of a partnership of love, trust and mutual support a higher emphasis in our modern marriage liturgies.

However, these ancient guides were clear-sighted about the potential of sexual desire to wreak havoc with human relationships and leave a trail of destruction in family and community life. So they counselled those who could not guarantee their self-control to seek out marriage.

I certainly believe that we need more than just a 'prevention from harm' rationale for marriage, indeed more too than the procreation rationale important though that is as well. However, the realism of the 'remedy against sin' line is a further rationale that does

---

20   Matthew 19:10–12 NIV
21   1 Corinthians 7:7
22   1 Corinthians 7:2,5,9

speak wisdom in a promiscuous society where desire is inflamed on many fronts and acted out in ways that leave many casualties not least the children whose homes are broken up by the instability of unfaithfulness. I well remember a conversation with the curate who ran the youth group I belonged to. I had been using in rather a super-spiritual way the single-minded and wholehearted disciple-ship argument for not going out with girls and he simply and play-fully commented 'David, I think you are the burning kind'. He was right, and I have been grateful for marriage to bring some order to those desires.

If we live in a society that constantly arouses sexual desire and exaggerates this dimension of relationship, and if for some that desire is felt towards those of the same-sex, and if celibacy is a gift only given to some, then it seems to me that there is a major injustice if the remedy offered to the heterosexual of channelling that desire into a faithful committed relationship is denied to the gay person. It is my serious pastoral encounters with a number of gay people that have helped me to feel the force of this. They want to be true both to the people they feel themselves to be and to live out a disciplined and responsible discipleship. A Church that simply offers the option of celibacy is failing to understand what they feel and need, which is to offer a sustainable and potentially holy way of life comparable to heterosexual marriage. Of course some gay people have embraced the path of celibacy and found fulfilment and peace in that choice. I know such people who have served God with distinction and courage. However, I do not believe either from the Scriptures or from my own experience that such is a calling for all gay people.

Taking Scripture Seriously

As an Evangelical I take the Scriptures very seriously and my argument so far has sought to interact with them. One of the key interpretative challenges of recent times has been to determine what the (comparatively few) references to homosexual behaviour in the Bible are actually referring to. Are the 'practising homosexuals' of 1 Corinthians 6:9 or I Timothy 1:10 in any way comparable to those living in faithful and committed relationships today? In the same way when looking at the connection in Romans 1 between idolatrous worship, same-sex relationships, and every kind of wickedness, evil, greed and depravity it is hard to see how the behaviour Paul is referring to equates to that of responsible gay Christians today. Is it not far more likely that promiscuity and religious prostitution are his actual targets?

While the understanding of such texts is important, for the purposes of this essay I have to refer you to the detailed discussion of them elsewhere. However, it is important to note what is happening in these particular discussions. The testimony of Scripture is having to interact with new facts and insights from human experience. The new reality demands a fresh look at traditional texts and understanding even as the latter seeks to shape the new experience into something authentically Christian. If loving and faithful same-sex relationships are a comparatively new phenomenon in the way they are lived out today, then we are not going to find much direct and explicit discussion of them in Scripture. However, what we can observe in Scripture is the process of the inclusion of new theological, pastoral and ethical insights, which in turn leads to the acceptance of new groups of people.

Lessons from the Early Church's Inclusion of the Gentiles

The greatest issue that the New Testament describes of this sort for the early Church is the inclusion of the Gentiles. Certain Jewish believers had insisted that salvation required circumcision for all alongside the keeping of the law of Moses. Paul and Barnabas were moved to disagree strongly with them, and so took their case to a meeting of the apostles and elders in Jerusalem. It is instructive to note what happens. First of all, they spent time noticing what God had been doing.[23] Paul and Barnabas are able to describe the evidence out in the field of what God had done through them among the Gentiles, revealing himself in remarkable ways as many were converted to the new faith. That provokes Simon Peter to recall the extraordinary occasion when he had been led through a sequence of visions and dreams to the Roman centurion Cornelius' house – entering it in a way that was unthinkable for a Jew. His previous ways of thinking had been radically challenged by an angel telling him: 'Do not call anything impure that God has made clean'.[24] He further describes how before he had even had a chance to finish his talk, the Holy Spirit had come upon his listeners as a sign of God's acceptance.

---

23   cf. Acts 15:4, 12–13
24   Acts 10:15

Then secondly they reflected on the Scriptures in the light of these things and of these things in the light of the Scriptures.[25] They realise that Peter's testimony chimes with the prophetic word of Amos – just one example of how the experience of the early church brought the Old Testament prophets to life – and of how new light is shed on the Scriptures as well as on what is happening among them as the two interact. So thirdly having noticed what God was doing, and reflected on it in the light of the Scriptures, they make a reasoned and grace-filled decision as expressed by James: 'It is my judgement, therefore, that we should not make it difficult for the Gentiles who are turning to God.' (v.19) So they refrain from demanding adherence to the Mosaic law and all its rituals only asking for certain points to be observed. Peter's argument has been persuasive when he suggests that they are testing God by 'putting on the necks of the Gentiles a yoke that neither we nor our ancestors have been able to bear'.

It would seem a pertinent question as to whether today the Church is putting on the necks of the gay community a yoke of celibacy that heterosexual people have been clearly unable to bear. Which of us can say that we have sexual desire and expression sorted and ordered in ways that are consistently healthy and loving even with the possibility of a committed and faithful relationship to explore such things? There appears to me a lack of empathy in some of the attitudes and stances taken by some Christians that denies the reality of what is really happening in relationships out there in society, and the complexity of their own sexuality. Sexual desire is both a precious gift for relational intimacy and a dangerous means of exploitation and abuse. I know that I have needed a committed relationship to channel this gift creatively. Do we deny gay people the same opportunity?

Furthermore, I believe that there is much that should be personal and private about setting the boundaries of intimacy as a couple seeks an appropriate expression of love within their relationship, and what is given or received as loving will vary greatly from person to person. Defining those boundaries in a rigid way would seem to me unhelpful and certainly for heterosexuals to be unduly prescriptive or judging of same-sex intimacy would seem to be inappropriate. I suspect that there have been many same-sex couples

---

25   Acts 15:15–18

living together over the years without the scrutiny of today's over sexualised imagination who have quietly lived their lives across a wide spectrum of friendship, love and intimacy.

Grace-Filled Wisdom – 'It seemed good to the Holy Spirit and to us...'

The Council of Jerusalem reached a point of decision about God's will for the Gentiles resolving not to make it unnecessarily difficult for them to join the Church. I look for similar grace-filled wisdom in relation to same-sex relationships. I love the phrase by which the apostles express their conclusions – 'It seemed good to the Holy Spirit and to us...' The words convey a measured wisdom and authority which reflects the fruit of an attentiveness to God combined with a mature human judgment. They had reflected on the new reality before them, listened to the Scriptures and discovered a way of grace that was permissive yet responsible, enabling yet disciplined and which opened them to an understanding and experience of God and the Scriptures that went far beyond their previous awareness.

I have not settled all the issues in my own mind about what that grace filled wisdom might look like for same-sex relationships. For instance, while I am sure that the expression of sexual intimacy within a faithful and committed relationship can be a loving, creative and holy option for gay people, I am not yet convinced that describing it as 'marriage' is helpful to the Christian tradition or to the unique sanctity and responsibility of procreation contained within it. I can understand gay people's longing for equality although I would argue for it being different from uniformity. So I am still on a journey, and understandings will no doubt continue to be shaped and developed as we reflect on experience and biblical models like covenanted partnerships. Sex is one of God's good gifts and it is a challenge today to keep it at the service of loving relationships. I hope that the church can move forward with imagination, integrity and grace-filled wisdom to enable that to happen for all God's people.

Chapter 9

Where You Go I Will Go

David Runcorn, Author and Speaker

The assumption tends to be made when an Evangelical is found speaking or writing in support of same-sex relationships that they must at some point have changed their minds. I never have. From my earliest awareness of the debates surrounding the Bible and homosexuality I struggled to be reconciled to conservative readings of the texts as applied to contemporary same-sex relationships. This was difficult because then, as now, I sought to shape my life and faith in obedience to the teachings of Scripture. The 'texts' and their interpretation appeared unequivocal. My understanding of biblical interpretation was very limited. But my unease would not go away.

When the Questions Are New

I am very grateful for the Evangelical tradition and the way it has shaped and nurtured my Christian life and faith. But it has not been an easy community in which to make the journey of thinking and questioning this context requires. All too often there was just nowhere to talk – as if no talk was needed on this issue. But one honourable exception to emerge in more recent years was Fulcrum – an 'open' evangelical website that for a time offered a lively (and rare) hospitable space to meet and discuss across real differences in an otherwise highly conflicted climate. It was there that the strands of an 'including' theology, based upon, not in spite of Scripture, finally began to come together for me.

The Evangelical tradition is still struggling with its response to same-sex relationships. One familiar response it makes to controversies of the day is to call Church and society *back* to things – Bible, Jesus. The intention is clear but I observe it is an instinctively conservative reflex. And where the challenges are significantly new and familiar texts do not immediately address them, it easily sounds defensive. But though it will take time one of the qualities of this tradition is its willingness to revise, reverse or adopt 'including' positions on social issues it previously opposed on scriptural grounds. The list includes slavery, apartheid, divorce and remarriage, contraception and women in society and Church. This is the challenge now facing it – though it is not clear what the outcome will be. But the unsettling process of faithful reading, re-examining, repenting, re-interpreting and revising even long unquestioned Biblical convictions under the compelling of the Spirit is a task this tradition knows well. We know Scripture itself requires it of us.

In the Pilling Report, to which I contributed an essay from an affirming Evangelical position,

Professor Oliver O'Donovan suggested there is something genuinely new about the ways in which homosexuality is being constructed and interpreted in contemporary society. Not surprisingly this is raising new and complex questions about the Church's understanding and response. He continues, 'it will require a great deal of straightforward observation, perhaps over several generations, before we can begin to answer any of these questions with confidence'.[26] I think he is right. Something new is going on. We haven't been here before. We are on a journey that requires trust, faith and commitment beyond our familiar boundaries.

The Stories We Bring

I am aware that what we bring to this conversation is influenced, in part, by the personal stories that have shaped us. I was educated in a single-sex private school. Images of homosexuality in that world swung between camp caricatures and drag acts to luridly speculative stories of furtive encounters in public toilets. In that educational culture male identity was formed around loyalty to the team, hierarchical authority, competition as character building, suspicion of feelings, despising of weakness and hostility to women. In fact, there was a terror of being thought feminine in any way. Changing room humour was relentlessly homophobic. In that world men could only publicly touch each other affectionately if they had first hit and insulted each, or after drinking too heavily to care. But nothing must imply any *actual* attraction of *that* sort. I note in passing that this was the formative educational environment for the greater percentage of the political, business and Church leaders in our society today (which remains substantially male). In my experience that brings its own challenges. And it is noticeable that, though the

---

26   Para 271

theological hard work still needs doing, the younger generation of Christians generally approach this debate with far less angst or anger, or are simply bewildered that it is an issue at all.

I first studied theology at London Bible College in the first flush of a renewed faith. That too was a patriarchal environment, conservative about sex, gender and life in general. But I noted how homosexuality drew very particular condemnation. It was *the* sin of sins: an 'Abomination'. Sodom gave its name to it. Romans 1 expounded it. It was the sign of end times. No further discussion was needed or expected. A deep, unspoken horror surrounded the very thought of 'it'. I was not sure why. Then in my second year a close, widely respected friend broke down when with me one evening and told me he was gay. I simply did not know what to say or how to respond. But I already knew of his faith and utter integrity. And I knew even then that his harrowed desires bore no resemblance to what this tradition presumed must be excluded as 'godless'. Then, as now, when you stop talking *about* and start talking *with* things have to change.

All the while I had my own journey to make towards emotional and social maturity as a white heterosexual man formed out of a relatively privileged upbringing, a conservative religion (for a time) and only slowly awakening to how much historic and social prejudice I had absorbed along the way. Disgust and embarrassment are not reliable measures of moral or biblical truth. But nowhere in my life and longings as a heterosexual Christian man was I obliged to hide from or deny who I was or what I desired, unless I chose to.

When I trained for ordination I had a close friend who was gay. It was the first time I had closely shared someone's personal journey of struggle and questioning. He became a vicar in London and a significant counsellor to the gay community there. Some years later when I was in personal crisis his friendship was a crucial gift. I have never forgotten the care with which he and his friends welcomed me in my brokenness. I have aspired to the same ever since. There was a quality of commitment and an integrity to their faith and relating that bore no resemblance I could see to the familiar readings of Romans 1, Sodom, or the more general pronouncements I heard from evangelical teachers. 'They' were simply not 'that'.

While a chaplain at the Lee Abbey community in Devon I discovered a small book of privately published prayers and meditations, *Prayer at Night.*[27] It contained the most original pastoral, spiritual and relationally aware reflections on the confusing, invariably wounded world of human sexual longing and belonging. They were transformative. Here was wisdom and healing for the challenges of embodied relational living. I sold so many copies to grateful guests that the curious author sought me out. And so began an important friendship with the late Jim Cotter – a pioneering minister who resourced so many of us in our present exploring. I still pray those prayers.

But I am continually reminded that for most of my gay friends, Church is a place they have to stay hidden – and in precisely those areas of their lives they are most vulnerable and needing support. They sense very quickly where they are safe. More often they struggle in private and their most significant friendships can never be enjoyed in public.

Faithful Improvising with the Word

The Bible is at the centre of this debate. Rightly so. But each tradition of the Church has its own ways of defining what this means. And each tends to believe their position to be the most reasonable and coherent, of course. It is the approach of the *others* we have questions about! The Evangelical tradition has its own passionate and particular devotion to the Bible that is not always easy for those outside to understand. In this context it means that if Scripture is believed to condemn same-sex relationships this is *primarily* a matter of obedience to what the Bible teaches. The criticism or scorn of others will not sway them. After all, doesn't the New Testament warn the followers of Christ to expect rejection? This is a *theological* issue. It needs to be addressed theologically. My conservative friends are right to insist on that – though it concerns me that this tradition has yet to really become aware of the impact of its teaching on those whose lives bear the weight and consequence of their beliefs.

Theologian Tom Wright likens the relationship of the Church to Scripture to the participation in a five-act play.[28] The Church's part is in the dynamic improvisation that forms the fifth act. As every actor

---

27 *Cairns for the Journey* – the last section of prayers in Jim Cotter's *Prayer at Night – A Book for the Darkness* (Cairns Publications, 2011)
28 Bishop NT Wright, *How Can the Bible be Authoritative?* (The Laing Lecture, 1989) http://ntwrightpage.com/Wright_Bible_Authoritative.htm

knows, to improvise faithfully requires a deep, obedient and sustained immersion in the first four acts. No one is making anything up. But this does challenge certain understandings of scriptural authority and assumptions of a single, controlling interpretation in the text which can then be simply applied to our own context.

Reading Scripture is also an invitation to join a conversation. The sheer diversity of voices and texts within the Bible means that readers of Scripture 'have their own work to do in discerning the unity of the story'.[29] One brief example must suffice here – the Book of Ruth. This short story of tragedy to new life is squeezed amongst the muscular, often violent narratives of Joshua and Judges. While policies of pitiless exclusion, slaughter and racial cleansing are being pursued in the name of God by his people, this story appears to stand in complete contradiction to the dominant scripts that surround it – culturally, relationally and theologically. It is a story of radical inclusion, matched by even more radical blessing by Yahweh. At its climax the most respected man in the community marries a foreign woman. The women of Bethlehem bless her in the name of their most revered spiritual mother, Rachel. She will become the great grandmother of Israel's greatest king. Where do we hear God speaking in these contrasting texts? If the Church contends with contradictory voices – so do its own Scriptures. Within the Scripture the word of the Lord is discerned in dialogue. The challenge, in any age, is how to read the Bible *wisely*.

When I read the Bible alongside the contemporary phenomena of faithful, committed same-sex relationships I hold two interpretative principles in mind. Firstly, 'Homosexuality' and 'Sexuality' are modern concepts. The words themselves are only found from the 19th century onwards. Bringing them into engagement with ancient texts where they are not to be known needs to be done with great care. Secondly, where the Bible texts refer to same-sex sexual activity and condemns it – as they always do – we must be as clear as possible about the concerns, contexts and intentions of the original writers. That means asking 'What *precisely* is being condemned here and *why*?' And 'what relevance does this text, and its apparent meaning, hold for understanding the contemporary expression of faithful committed same-sex love as we know it today? My conviction continues to grow that when that happens the texts no longer

---

29   Richard Bauckham, quoted in Karl Allen Kuhn, *Having Words with God – the Bible as Conversation* (Augsburg Fortress, Minneapolis 2008) p13

support the conservative reading on same-sex attraction in the way so long presumed.

Crossing the Boundaries

There are words spoken in a defining moment in the story of Ruth which express so much of what I aspire to in our present context. As Naomi returns home to her own people she tries to send her foreign daughters in law away. Ruth refuses to go. 'Where you go I will go, your people shall be my people, your God, my God', she says (1.16–17). In her commitment to Naomi, Ruth crosses some of the dangerous boundaries in her time – racial, cultural, religious, relational. She becomes a bridge builder. At considerable personal risk, she modelled a different way of being and belonging. Furthermore, her offer was not welcomed. But she persisted. So a journey that began with the offer and rejection of love and companionship, ends in inclusion, celebration and new community.[30]

Those verses are often read at weddings – they were at mine. They said what we wanted to say to each other. But they are not about marriage. We were borrowing from another expression of committed relationship to express what we aspired to in our own.

I want to reciprocate that borrowing. I want other expressions of committed relationships to receive the same support, delight and gifts that I know my marriage has received. I long for the sustaining of the varied vocations to faithful, human loving in our world for the enriching of the whole. I am so grateful to those who, like Ruth, have offered, stayed, persisted, endured rejection and isolation in a socially and ethically conservative Church and so have become sources of renewing, partnership and grace to all. And I mourn those for whom the cost was too great.

It seems to me that if, in the Kingdom for which we pray daily, there is neither male nor female nor, ultimately, marriage, then other ways of relating and belonging are opened up. Even the creation injunction to 'Be fruitful and multiply' is no longer for understanding as only procreation within heterosexual marriage. Sex is not just about fertility and children. And if celibacy (as only very briefly expounded in the New Testament: 1Cor7) can now be chosen as a fruitful expression of discipleship in a community whose life points

---

30 Given the capacity of this subject for misunderstanding I take the precaution of stating that I am *not* saying Ruth and Naomi were in a same-sex relationship

to the coming Kingdom, might not other patterns of committed, non-procreative relationship be possible too? There are, and always have been, other patterns of fruitful human belonging – and thank God for that. However well intended there has been an Evangelical focus on marriage that has placed a heavy burden on marriage itself as well as treating so many other forms of relating as somehow incomplete.

Taste and See

When I say that I meet Christ and see the Spirit at work in the lives of my single and partnered gay friends I can be criticised for putting my experience above the authority of Scripture. This is a very particularly Evangelical concern. But Jesus himself teaches the test of experience. 'By their fruits you shall recognise them … a good tree cannot bear bad fruit'. (Matt 7.16–18). What is often missed is that there are two sides to applying the test of fruit. There is the evidence of positive, good fruit of the life and faith of Christians who happen to be gay. I see that everywhere. But there is also the bitter fruit that has been the result of excluding teaching and behaviour in the Church towards gay people. This needs real honesty. The damage has been huge but often hidden.

The challenge of this test is that fruit needs time to grow and reveal its quality. You cannot know beforehand – particularly if it is fruit you have not known before, or perhaps did not even plant yourself. This must be a longer-term strategy for discernment. Furthermore, you cannot grow fruit at a distance. It requires our willingness to be directly and positively involved in the nurturing and growing process. Fruit requires tending, care and feeding. This test calls us to patient and non-anxious inclusion within a trusting theology of time.

I am grateful for shared conversations and any initiatives that create listening spaces to meet, talk and understand each other better. When the search for love, belonging and intimacy is happening in a society without moral compass, and where familiar boundaries for human relating have all but collapsed, the journey towards intimacy of any kind may be a very difficult one. It can easily become an experience of great wounding, hurt and bewilderment. To engage in this debate at all is to enter a place of intense vulnerability and often profound pain. It must take the time it takes and can only proceed as we are able and willing. To start at the place of 'right' or 'wrong' is unhelpful and ultimately unproductive. Real lives are involved here. The response of Jesus in the place of human brokenness was to call for mercy not sacrifice.

In the midst of such a society it would be wonderful if the Church could become a community living together without fear. Where the varied human vocations to friendship, love and commitment are hallowed, celebrated, and held within the nurturing boundaries of holy trust and covenant. The choice (or call) to live as celibate will be understood and reverenced here also.

The Christian Church is to be a sign of the Kingdom. We live in anticipation of a life that is 'breaking-in' from the future. We pray with longing for its coming. We are forward looking people – communities continually being called into the newness that is the vision of God in Christ. Faithful living involves risk, choice, adventure, exploration, stepping into the unknown and living beyond the familiar. We are on a journey we have not been on before. But I believe it to be towards a new community that that Jesus is calling us to become. I find myself journeying alongside people who for too long have been excluded and presumed to be outside the story, and to them I want to say: 'where you, go I will go, your people will be my people, your God, my God.' (Ruth 1.16,17)

Chapter 10

Making Space for Truth and Grace

James Jones, Former Bishop of Liverpool

This personal essay was originally written when Bishop James was Bishop of Liverpool for 'A Fallible Church' edited by Kenneth Stevenson, published by DLT January 2008

However else you may wish to define and describe the Anglican Communion the reality is that it consists of myriad relationships between Dioceses, Deaneries, Parishes and Provinces around the globe. Like a map from an in-flight magazine that shows the airline's routes criss-crossing the world so the Anglican Church offers a network of links that connect people from different cultures. It lacks the structured pattern of a spider's web because these connecting strands do not emerge from the strategic planning department of a central secretariat. Rather it resembles a spilled bowl of spaghetti! This image is not to belittle the Communion but to recognise that the shapelessness of the Communion is part of its history and its character.

Although there have been attempts to order and to organise the Communion the reality is that Dioceses, Deaneries and Parishes have over the years exercised great freedom in entering into relationships with one another. And again, although guidelines exist to steer these partnerships the fact is they are shaped much more by need, experience, enthusiasm and friendship. It means that whatever formal relationships exist between Primates and Provinces there exists at another level an untidy yet surprisingly strong set of mature relationships that have stood the test of time. The Diocese of Liverpool has been in formal partnerships with two other Dioceses – Akure and Virginia. The driving force behind me initiating a tripartite conversation on sexuality was the idea that the debate about contentious subjects is best located in already established relationships. It is better to deal with difficult ethical and doctrinal questions – in this case, sexuality – in a conversation between people who already know, trust and respect each other than through megaphone diplomacy between strangers across the oceans. The historic partnerships within the Anglican Communion can offer a different context for the debate about homosexuality where there can be a genuine dialogue between people whose mutual trust and affection protect them from jumping too soon to conclusions and keep them in conversation because a long time ago they learned to think the best and not the worst of each other.

One of the things that happens when conversations begin especially when they involve more than two people is that you begin to see that there are more than two sides to an argument. In a media dominated world everything is polarised in a most reductionist way and even the most complex issues reduced to whether you are for or against a particular subject. This treatment does not do justice to the complexity of ethical discourse and ill serves the people most affected by the debate. One of the discoveries I found in our conversation about homosexuality between the continents of Africa, Europe and America is that there was a variety of insights, perspectives and opinions that defied the way the media polarise the debate into simply two clear-cut oppositional positions and want always to reduce complex and nuanced positions into the half-truths of soundbites. This is not to deny that in the end an ethical decision has to be taken. What it recognises is that there needs to be more space along the way for people to view the terrain from different vantage points. But it is difficult to maintain this space especially under pressure from the world-wide media whose tendency is to dramatise, to polarise and to present every issue in terms of extreme opposites. This is not the place for an essay on the media, and there is much that is good about a communications industry that has raised international public awareness of global poverty and the environment. But one of the tensions that Christians struggle with in the modern world is that we live and move and have our being in a globe saturated by media that drive people apart through this polarising tendency and produce a dynamic in human relationships at odds with the reconciling and unifying movement of the Gospel.

Some will point to our history and to the Scriptures for the need to act decisively and will interpret this plea for space as a lack of courage and leadership. What I have found in our tripartite conversation is that the space has yielded new insights, not least because that space has been protected by an established relationship in Christ of trust and affection.

In Acts 15 the Council of Jerusalem was dogged in a controversy. What was at stake was the essence of the Gospel. There was dissension and debate about the means of salvation. This was a first order issue. Some Christians were insisting that salvation required the Gentile converts to be circumcised. 'Unless you are circumcised according to the custom of Moses, you cannot be saved' (15:1). What I find of special significance for how Christians handle controversy is that Luke describes these detractors as 'believers'. Even though the doctrine they were proposing undermined the doctrine of grace and of justification through faith the author included them within the body of believers. Within that space there was heated debate as they wrestled for the truth. This example has informed my own attitude and practice when it comes to theological and ethical debates, offering and in turn hoping for a generosity of spirit and the space to question and to listen to different interpretations and experiences of both first and second order issues.

It also makes me quizzical about the talk of 'impaired communion' which itself seems to undermine the doctrine of grace and certainly shrinks the space within which to have frank theological debate.

We are in Christ by the grace of God. None of us earns or merits that place. In Christ we find ourselves alongside and at one (whether we like it – or them – or not) with all others who by God's grace are also in Christ. We cannot take ourselves into Christ, neither can we remove another from being in Christ. It is all by grace. Now it is clear that controversy can impair friendship, can affect ministry and even undermine mission but only Christ can determine communion, with him and through him with one another. As in the Council of Jerusalem and the controversy over doctrine and practice so today in the Anglican Communion there may be impaired mission, impaired ministry, impaired friendship but as to 'communion' that is only and forever in and through Christ alone.

These are the sentiments that have informed the debate about human sexuality in the Diocese of Liverpool and encouraged us to take the initiative to discuss it with our partner Dioceses.

Within the Diocese of Liverpool I called for the debate to be set within a new framework, within a forum of four walls, recognising that each of the four sides is a vital part of the forum of discussion.

The first point of the quadrilateral is to recognise the authoritative Biblical emphasis upon the uniqueness of marriage as a divine ordinance for the ordering of human society and the nurture of children.

The second is to acknowledge the authoritative Biblical examples of love between two people of the same gender most notably in the relationship of Jesus and his beloved and David and Jonathan.

The third is to register the role of conscience in the Anglican moral tradition; in the Church of England's oaths of canonical obedience the vow is to be obedient 'in all things lawful and honest' which means that should you be pressed to do something which in good conscience you deem not to be honest then conscience would demand that you dissent.

The fourth point is to understand that disunity saps the energy of the Church and to affirm the importance of unity to the mission of God. Each of these sides merits closer inspection and deserves its own essay. But the point I want to make is that holding these four together has produced space within the Diocese for us to have a genuine conversation.

The 1998 Lambeth Conference asked us to be in dialogue with gay and lesbian people and as a result of that in 2001 I invited Professor Ian Markham then Professor of Public Theology at Liverpool Hope University and now Dean of Virginia Theological Seminary to chair a group exploring 'A Theology of Friendship'. The group's membership reflected the diversity of opinion, theological, ethical and ecclesiastical and was inclusive of gender. The group worked for two years with occasional residential consultations and needed all that time to build trust so that honest discussion could take place. Although I was not part of the group my own thinking has been informed by their findings. In particular I have continued to reflect on the biblical material. The quality of the group's work has set the tone for the debate in the Diocese which is an important contribution to our common life and to the mission of God, for energy is not being sapped by internal strife.

The Theology of Friendship Report took me in particular to the relationship between David and Jonathan. Their friendship was emotional, spiritual and even physical. Jonathan loved David 'as his own soul'. David found Jonathan's love for him, 'passing the love of women'. There was between them a deep emotional bond that left David grief-stricken when Jonathan died. But not only were they emotionally bound to each other they expressed their love physically. Jonathan stripped off his clothes and dressed David in his own robe and armour. With the candour of the Eastern World that exposes the reserve of Western culture they kissed each other and wept openly with each other. The fact that they were both married did not inhibit them in emotional and physical displays of love for each other. This intimate relationship was sealed before God. It was not just a spiritual bond it became covenantal for 'Jonathan made a covenant with David, because he loved him as his own soul' (1 Samuel 18:3). Here is the Bible bearing witness to love between two people of the same gender. I know that at this point some will ask, 'Was the friendship sexual?', 'Were they gay?', 'Was at least one of them homosexual?', 'Were they both heterosexual?', 'Were they bisexual?' I want to resist these questions at least initially. Immediately you start using such words you conjure up stereotypes and prejudices. Further, you assume that it is a person's sexual inclination that defines their personhood. Is it not possible to say that here are two men with the capacity to love fully, both women and men?

The intimacy between David and Jonathan is also evident in the relationship between the Son of David and his beloved John. We find the two at one with each other during the supper when Jesus washes the feet of his disciples. The beloved disciple is found reclining next to Jesus. Translations are not adequate to the text. Two different phrases are used in verses 23 and 25. One of them says literally that John was leaning against the bosom, breast, chest of Jesus (*kolpos*).

No English word or phrase fully captures the closeness of the liaison. What is significant is that the word used in John 13:23 is found only on one other occasion in the Gospel of John. In John 1:18 the word is used to describe the intimate relationship between 'God the only Son' and the Father. 'No one has ever seen God. It is God the only Son who is close to the Father's heart (*kolpos*) who has made him known'. It is difficult for a human being to conceive of a closer relationship than that between the Persons of the Holy Trinity. That this word is used of the relationship between Jesus and John is a remarkable expression of the love between the two men. This love finds expression on several occasions. On the cross

Jesus makes his beloved friend his mother's son in an extraordinary covenant of love and on the day of the Resurrection love propels the bereaved and beloved disciple to outrun Peter and arrive first at the Tomb. Here is energising love, spiritual, emotional and physical.

It is with reflections such as these that I entered with anticipation into the dialogue with our partner Dioceses within the Anglican Communion. I also came as we all do to every encounter with a history. I had been one of the nine Diocesan Bishops to have objected publicly to the proposed consecration of Dr Jeffrey John, now Dean of St Albans. I deeply regret this episode in our common life. I regret too having objected publicly without first having consulted with the Archbishops of York and Canterbury and subsequently apologised to them and to colleagues in a private meeting of the House of Bishops. I still believe that it was unwise to try to take us to a place that evidently did not command the broad support of the Church of England but I am sorry for the way I opposed it and I am sorry too for adding to the pain and distress of Dr John and his partner. I regret too that this particular controversy narrowed rather than enlarged the space for healthy debate within the Church.

I have wrestled with writing the above for fear of opening old wounds but I cannot give a true account of my part in the continuing debate without acknowledging the history I brought to the table. In the same way (and they must speak for themselves) the Bishops and correspondents from Africa and America needed to acknowledge their own stories in coming to the conversation.

We have had two residential conferences within the tripartite conversation. In April 2005 Liverpool invited Akure and in November 2006 invited both Akure and Virginia. Agreed statements describe the process and the substance of our reflections to which I am not at liberty to add. In each case the conversation was facilitated by Stephen Lyon whose skills added indisputably to the quality of the conversation.

These encounters in England together with my own visits to America and Africa have enabled me to study the Scriptures with greater cultural awareness. I have a deeper and more affectionate understanding of both Africa and America. I can see how the Church of Nigeria's response to the sexuality debate is contextualised. The law of their land prohibits homosexual acts. It is therefore difficult for the Church to be party to an international debate about a practice that is actually outlawed and illegal. Whatever moral view one takes and however much one denounces the persecution and oppression that has ensued it is possible to acknowledge the challenge of their cultural context. Furthermore, in Africa as elsewhere in the world there is a battle with Islam for the hearts and minds of the masses of the population. African Christianity wants to guard itself from the charge that it is a front for Western Imperialism in decadent decline. Associating with the agenda and sexual mores of American and European societies allows Christianity's Islamic critics to portray the Church in Africa as compromised, weak and in moral decline. These are serious missiological issues which need to be recognised and understood, rather than pilloried and dismissed.

The same is true for America where the proposers of change are also subject to caricature. The Civil Rights movement has a much greater grip on the soul of America than it does on either England or Europe generally.

For many in the Episcopal Church the rights of gay and lesbian people are seen unequivocally akin to the rights of African-Americans. There is a poignant irony here for it is with Africans from contemporary Africa that many American Episcopalians are most at odds in a cause that they feel parallels the plight of and the fight for justice by their ancestors who came to America two centuries earlier. Gay rights are civil rights. It is a matter of natural justice. Failure to understand this at best mystifies and at worst angers the majority in the Episcopal Church that was once so guiltily complicit in slavery and is now so anxious to shake off the shackles of the past and prove its commitment to social justice which is such an important strand in the prophetic literature of the Bible. These are serious historical and contemporary moral and social perspectives that need to be understood in the international debate about human sexuality.

What I have learned from our tripartite conversation is that we need to have and protect the space for genuine dialogue in the spirit of Lambeth 1:10. I worry about the Windsor proposals not because I doubt the courage and integrity of those who are working on them but because I fear that they will take us in the direction of narrowing the space and of closing down the debate on this and any future issue where Christians find themselves in conversation with their culture on some new moral development or dilemma. The result is that energy is sapped by internal definitions rather than released into engaging with the world so loved of God.

The description in John's Gospel of Jesus 'full of grace and truth' presents us with a person who created space around himself for others to 'see the Kingdom of God'. He was neither truthless in his grace, nor graceless in his truth. I fear that in our debates with each other and with the world especially on the subject of homosexuality we have come over as graceless. Jesus was a pastor, as well as a prophet. He spoke commandments with compassion. And when in John 8 he was asked to judge an adulterer he said 'Neither do I condemn you' before adding 'Go away and sin no more'. The Pastor spoke before the Prophet. Had it been the other way around she would not have been there to hear his words of mercy. I am not here equating homosexuality with adultery but simply registering the priority Jesus gave to the pastoral approach.

I know there are some – from all sides of the argument – who might feel that to be in conversation with those with whom you profoundly disagree is to legitimise their own position and compromise your own. I know too that the continuing debate does not alleviate the suffering of those most affected. In this time, we are particularly dependent on the grace of those who are hurt by the words and actions of others. All I know and can testify to through our own discussions within the Diocese and with our partner Dioceses is that entering the debate prayerfully in the company of the One who is 'full of grace and truth' takes you to places beyond 'all that you can ask or imagine'. I know that many are pessimistic about the future but I find myself strangely and surprisingly optimistic that if we can maintain the space to listen to 'the still small voice' there might emerge a new understanding and paradigm that none of us can yet imagine.

APPENDIX

Open Table

Kieran Bohan and Warren Hartley

St Bride's Liverpool relaunched in November 2007 with a vision for a 'creative, progressive, inclusive' community. Open Table is a Fresh Expression which began shortly afterwards, in July 2008, as a manifestation of this vision.

It takes the form of a monthly service, usually a Eucharist, which aims to create a safe, sacred space with a warm and affirming welcome for Liverpool's Lesbian, Gay, Bisexual and Transgender (LGBT) community, who have traditionally not been well served by mainstream church. Our primary goal is to explore faith amongst LGBT Christians, and assist them in integrating their spiritual and sexual identities – as for some these have been in direct conflict. We also welcome and affirm family members, friends and other allies who also seek an inclusive Church community.

An early member once asked us: 'Will it be "open table"?' Sadly, this is because LGBT Christians have often either felt or been intentionally excluded from the Eucharist.

Following conversations with our then Bishop, our Rector and other supportive clergy, Open Table began in July 2008 with a mix of Anglicans, Roman Catholics, URC and Methodist folk. In 2012 St Bride's District Church Council formalised the Open Table leadership by creating the role of LGBT Ministry Facilitator – which Warren undertook with Kieran's support. Open Table has grown from a gathering of around half a dozen or so in 2008 to regularly drawing up to 40 people each month.

To create this sacred space which has a real sense of God's presence where all can 'come as you are', we have explored liturgy, carefully choosing resources and constructing services that affirm our identity as children of God.

Over time, regulars expressed a desire to get to know each other beyond the limits of a monthly service. This led to the invitation to regather, after post-service refreshments, for a 'sharing circle', which now takes place most months. We introduce this as a time for holding one another in prayerful attention; not a therapy or discussion group, but rather an opportunity for deep and respectful listening to any who wish to share what is going on in their lives and spiritual journeys. If anyone wants to respond to anything shared during this time, we invite them to reach out outside the sharing circle. This is well received, attracting up to 16 or so people each time.

Some have expressed a desire to go deeper in knowledge of faith, the Scriptures and our identities as LGBT people. This has led to us running two house groups which meet regularly for a meal, study and spiritual practice, using the Inclusive Church resource 'Living Christianity' to reflect on the Eucharist over seven weeks. We have also facilitated two retreat days looking at what it means to be LGBT and Christian, as individuals and as a community. One of the recommendations that emerged from this is that we seek to develop liturgies to mark important life events, e.g. a coming out service, an affirmation of gender transition, services of thanksgiving (and, we hope and pray, perhaps eventually blessings) for civil partnerships and marriages.

We regularly celebrate the feasts of the Church calendar, and key dates in the LGBT calendar, including LGBT History Month (February), International Day Against Homophobia, Biphobia and Transphobia (May), Liverpool Pride (August), and Transgender Day of Remembrance (November). These services are often 'services of the word' led by members of the community. We share the importance of our testimonies as LGBT people and as Christians, and we stand in solidarity with our LGBT sisters and brothers around the world who do not share the same freedom we enjoy. This has been so important in empowering sometimes deeply hurt and vulnerable people.

Members of Open Table, and the wider St Bride's community, have walked alongside other inclusive faith communities in the Liverpool Pride march, and shared a community stall during the festival, since it began in 2010. This has often been in partnership with Spectrum of Spirituality, an LGBT Interfaith Forum established in 2010, to host an annual Interfaith service as part of the official Pride Festival, the first of its kind in the UK.

It is a delight to see other Open Table ministries emerging – there are currently active groups in Warrington, Manchester and north

Wales, with enquiries from six other communities nationally. Each is independent, but we offer peer support, encouragement and learning from our experience.

With little dedicated Christian ministry for them, many LGBT people seek spirituality elsewhere, particularly within Buddhism as it is perceived to be more LGBT affirming. The Open Table model is therefore an important outreach opportunity that witnesses to an inclusive gospel. Together with a positive Christian presence at Pride and other community events, , we hope to challenge negative perceptions of Christianity among the LGBT community. In addition, we are keen to offer training and support opportunities to other Christian communities who are open to exploring issues of sexuality, gender identity and spirituality.

It is worth noting that estimates of the size of the LGBT population vary widely from 1.5% (Office of National Statistics 2011) to as high as 10% (Spiegelhalter, *Sex By Numbers,* 2012). Even if we take the lower figure as accurate, there are approximately over 24,000 LGBT people within the Diocese of Liverpool – a significant number with whom to share Christian faith and spirituality.

Our hope for Open Table is that we can be a place where LGBT people and others can meet God, the source of life, love and being and thus come to know that they are beloved children of God. Through that encounter we ourselves are transformed, and become agents of transformation in an imperfect world. As LGBT people, we believe our lives, our identities and our relationships are precious gifts from God, which we are called to live out with integrity. Our desire is to continue to build a community where this is evident and which equips others to go out and do the same.

Warren Hartley and Kieran Bohan are a lay couple,
formally authorised as Local Missional Leaders
in the Diocese of Liverpool

POSTSCRIPT

Cindy Kent, Broadcaster

I am totally in favour of women Priests. Well, I would be, wouldn't I, since I am one! But I didn't always feel this way. About 25 years ago I didn't think it was possible. No, to be a Priest you had to be a man, because Jesus was a man and a man was the head of the family etc. etc. All my life the leaders of any church I'd attended had been a man. And that was the way it was meant to be. End of. However, around that time I started interviewing people on the radio for a living and talked to people on both sides of the debate. I began to realise more and more that I was thinking the way I did mainly because of tradition. That's all I'd ever known – but the more I thought about it; prayed about it and talked to people from the differing 'pro' and 'anti' sides I began to change my mind.

And that's how I feel about the vexed issue of Christians and their sexuality. Coming from a show business background I was used to having gay and lesbian friends and I never thought twice about whether they should be singers/actors/record producers etc. That's who – and what – they were – and still are. Bill was a song publisher, and a very good one, and the fact that he was gay never came into the equation. And then I wondered how I would feel about Bill being a Priest. And I got the same answer. God made Bill and was using him as a whole person – personality, flaws, failings and faith – all contributed to making Bill Bill.

I have had many discussions over the years with Evangelical Christians about believing every word that's in the Bible. I interviewed one prominent (American) Pastor who, when I asked whether he really believed that Balaam's ass spoke said, yes he had to. If he questioned the veracity of that, then he would have to question everything else that was in the Bible. The acclaimed Christian veteran broadcaster, the Rev David Winter, in his book *But This I Can Believe* (Hodder & Stoughton, 1980) said 'It is a positively enriching thing to be released from a narrow, literalist view of the Bible to see it as it is, a dynamic Word, speaking as eloquently to modern man in his technology as it did to ancient man in his 'tents'. And that's the whole point surely? The Bible is a living Word. There are so many rules in it that we, as Christians, don't keep any more.

At the moment I'm wearing a polyester and viscose t-shirt – mixing two types of fabric together which the book of Leviticus tells me I shouldn't. Neither should I eat the fat of ox, sheep, or goat. And don't get me started on shellfish! And there are countless other rules and regulations which I break every single day.

There's always a problem though about quoting from Leviticus. We, as Christians, are no longer 'under the Law'. I certainly don't live my Christian life by following the Old Testament Law for if I did I would be 'under a curse' according to St Paul in his letter to the Galatians.

Let's stick with Paul for a while. He says – but *if* you are led by the Spirit, you are *not* under law. I guess that means that you cannot be bound by the Law and walk in the Spirit at the same time. In that same letter Paul says that we are free in Christ, and that 'we are freed from the yoke of slavery' (Galatians 5:1). And slavery is an interesting thought.

There was a time when it was considered totally ok to 'own a slave' –in fact there's plenty of verses from the Bible to back it up. Something which we now condemn. in the film *Amazing Grace* I was struck by the scene where, in 18th century England, William Wilberforce and William Pitt met up with and actual slave. They began to talk to each other and things began to change. And if that sounds like a romantic view of what really happened, then so be it. But I bet there's a grain of truth in it. When we start to talk to someone who is different from us, then things aren't quite so black and white. In fact, I remember someone in my congregation telling me that she had always been against homosexuality until she found out that her son was gay.

A few years ago I interviewed Gene Robinson on the *Breakfast Show* on Premier Christian Radio, where I worked for nearly 20 years. A brave step for them and for him. He knew what his audience would be like. I trod very carefully – and he was very honest. It was live and I had several emails and texts roundly condemning me to hell and back (only not quite put like that), and the stations for giving this man air space. However – there was one email which was very short and to the point. 'Thank you', it said, 'for what you've done for the LGBT community today'. Sadly, I guess that person finds little to encourage or help in many Christian publications – or churches – and maybe sits in a pew each week afraid to express their sexuality.

I take heart in the fact that there is nothing I can do today to make God love me more and there is nothing I can do to make God love me less.

The Church I belong to needs to be accepting and inclusive in order to be complete. God is a God of Love – in all its many and varied forms – and if two people love one another then where there's God, there's Love.

BIBLIOGRAPHY

The following books and essays are referenced by contributors within this book:

Achtemeier, Mark. *The Bible's Yes to Same-Sex Marriage – An Evangelical's Change of Heart* (Westminster John Knox Press, Louisville, 2014)

Boswell, John. *Christianity, Social Tolerance and Homosexuality* (University of Chicago Press, Chicago, 1980)

Brownson, James. *Bible, Gender and Sexuality – Reframing the Church's Debate on Same-Sex Relationships* (Eerdmans, Michigan, 2013)

Cotter, Jim. *Prayer at Night – A Book for the Darkness* (Cairns Publications, 2011)

Hollenweger, Walter. *Evangelism Today: Good News or Bone of Contention?* (Christian Journals Ltd, Belfast, 1976)

John, Jeffrey. *Permanent, Faithful, Stable* (Darton, Longman and Todd, 2012, new edn)

Kuhn, Karl Allen. *Having Words with God – Reading the Bible as Conversation* (Augsburg Fortress, Minneapolis, 2008)

Runcorn, David. *Appendix 4 – Evangelicals, Scripture and Same-Sex Relationships, Report of the House of Bishops – Working Group on Human Sexuality* ('The Pilling Report') (Church House Publishing, 2013)

Wright, NT. *How Can the Bible be Authoritative?* (The Laing Lecture 1989, originally published in *Vox Evangelica*, 1991)

Church of England Reports referenced within this book are:

General Synod Board for Social Responsibility: Homosexual Relationships – A Contribution to Discussion ('The Gloucester Report') (Church Information Office, London, 1979)

Issues in Human Sexuality – A Statement by the House of Bishops (Church House Publishing, London, 1991)

Report of the House of Bishops – Working Group on Human Sexuality ('The Pilling Report') (Church House Publishing, London, 2013)

Other books written by evangelicals that explain how they have come to an affirming mindset:

Gushee, David. *Changing Our Mind* (David Crumm Media, Michigan, 2014)

Lee, Justin. *Unconditional – Rescuing the Gospel from the Gays-vs-Christians Debate* (Hodder & Stoughton, London, 2014)

Marks, Jeremy. *Exchanging the Truth of God for a Lie* (Courage UK, Walton-on-Thames, 2008)

Vasey, Michael. *Strangers and Friends: A New Exploration of Homosexuality and the Bible* (Hodder & Stoughton, London, 1995)

Vines, Matthew. *God and the Gay Christian: The Biblical Case in Support of Same-Sex Relationships* (Convergent Books, New York, 2014)

Wilson, Ken. *A Letter to My Congregation* (David Crumm Media, Michigan, 2014)

ABOUT VIA MEDIA PUBLICATIONS

This book has been produced under the full and final editorial control of Via Media Publications, in collaboration with the contributors.

Via Media Publications is part of ViaMedia.News (https://viamedia.news/), a weekly blog that has the backing of a range of senior figures in the Church of England in order to prompt a deeper level of reflection.

Edited by Jayne Ozanne, the website aims to bring the historic Anglican perspective of the 'Via Media' (or 'Middle Way') to debates that are current in the Church and wider world. It features contributions from a range of influential Anglicans as they seek to bring a fresh perspective to areas of controversy, and so attempt to bridge the divides that separate many within the Church.

ABOUT EKKLESIA

Ekklesia, which is publishing this book for Via Media, is a Christian think tank advocating transformative theological ideas in the public square. Its core values are deeply rooted in scripture and tradition. Ekklesia holds that there are solid biblical and theological reasons for supporting same-sex relationships, and seeks to promote the voices of evangelicals and others articulating that view within a Christian debate, which needs to be faithful and honest.